INSPI

Sivananda Yoga Vedanta Centre
51 Felsham Road, London SW15 1AZ
Tel 020 8780-0160 Fax 020 8780-0128
e-mail; London@sivananda.org

Yoga classes, books,
tapes, mail order

INSPIRING STORIES

SRI SWAMI SIVANANDA

Published By

THE DIVINE LIFE SOCIETY

P.O. Shivanandanagar—249 192

Distt. Tehri-Garhwal, Uttaranchal, Himalayas, India

Price | **2005**   [85/-

First Edition:	1963
Second Edition:	1980
Third Edition:	1983
Fourth Edition:	1989
Fifth Edition:	1994
Sixth Edition:	1997
Seventh Edition:	2005

[2,000 Copies]

ISBN 81-7052-030-4

Published by Swami Vimalananda for
The Divine Life Society, Shivanandanagar, and printed by him
at the Yoga-Vedanta Forest Academy Press,
P.O. Shivanandanagar, Distt. Tehri-Garhwal, Uttaranchal,
Himalayas, India

UNIVERSAL PRAYER

O adorable Lord of mercy and love,
Salutations and prostrations unto Thee;
Thou art omnipresent, omnipotent and omniscient;
Thou art Satchidananda;
Thou art the Indweller of all beings.

> *Grant us an understanding heart,*
> *Equal vision, balanced mind,*
> *Faith, devotion and wisdom;*
> *Grant us inner spiritual strength to resist*
> *temptations*
> *And to control the mind;*
> *Free us from egoism, lust, greed, anger and*
> *hatred;*
> *Fill our hearts with divine virtues.*

Let us behold Thee in all these names and forms,
Let us serve Thee in all these names and forms,
Let us ever remember Thee,
Let us ever sing Thy glories,
Let Thy Name be ever upon our lips,
Let us abide in Thee for ever and ever.

—Swami Sivananda

PUBLISHERS' PREFACE

Teachers of subtle truths have always employed the story form of instruction to impart to students knowledge of realms beyond the ken of human perception and intricate aspects of philosophy as well as crucial lessons in ethics and the way of moral living. Worshipful Sri Gurudev Swami Sivanandaji Maharaj was always fond of employing this method of spiritual and ethical instruction for bringing about spiritual awakening in people. Swamiji has written several such books of instructive and illuminating stories, among which the present volume entitled 'INSPIRING STORIES' forms a very valuable book of guidance upon right conduct, philosophic thinking, human psychology and spiritual life in general. As such, it will be an invaluable addition to the personal library of students eager to know more about the secrets of life on earth and life beyond.

Sri Swami Sivanandaji Maharaj, as an exemplary Sannyasin, was one of those stalwarts in the spiritual field who considered the spirit of renunciation in a world of phantasmal presentations as of paramount importance. One would find that in all his writings there is an under-current of 'renunciation'. Though he has tirelessly attempted in his various writings to present even to the novitiate the true meaning of this supremely requisite qualification, namely, renunciation, one can safely conclude that there is no feature of spiritual life more misunderstood, misconstrued and misinterpreted than the demand for renunciation as a response to the call of the higher life. The illusion before the eyes of man is so inscrutably constructed that not even the wisest of people have found it easy to extricate themselves from its powerful clutches penetrating into the very vitals of one's being. This insistence on an interesting and important factor in the leading of the truly spiritual life is to be considered the explanation for this book commencing, at the outset, with a not-much-known but awakening message through the very first story.

Though the nature of these stories, parables and anecdotes is basically oriented from the point of view of a noble spiritual life, they will also serve definitely the useful purpose of being suitable non-detailed texts that may be prescribed in educational institutions.

Shivanandanagar,   —THE DIVINE LIFE SOCIETY

CONTENTS

1

CITY OF BENIGHTEDNESS

THIS PHENOMENAL world is a realm of sense perceptions. The mind and the senses are extremely deceptive and unreliable. Therefore all appearances and experiences perceived through them are totally misleading and dangerously deluding. All things seemingly appear to be going one way but turn out to be quite different later on. The painful puts on the garb of the pleasant, whereas the evil masquerades beneath goodness. This is the inscrutable game of Maya. One who deeply reflects upon this and understands it well walks in the path of light. He who succumbs to this deception comes to dwell in the "City of Benightedness" and leads a precarious life that lands him into endless trouble. Real blessedness lies in the Self. The sense-world constitutes the direct antitheses or total contradiction of the Self. In the Self alone abide eternal life and lasting bliss, whereas sensual indulgence is a poison that destroys life. Listen to this interesting story.

There was once a wandering monk and his disciple. The monk was wise and vigilant. The young disciple was impetuous and at times foolhardy, due to his love of pleasure.

1

During their wanderings they once arrived at the city of a king named Rajarajeshwar Brihat-moodh Bahadur. The city was called Andhernagari. Putting up at a rest-house, the Guru sent the disciple to purchase some foodstuffs from the bazaar for their frugal meal. The disciple went but soon returned, dancing in glee and loaded with a big bagful of eatables, sweets and fruits of endless variety. The Guru asked him what all this meant.

The disciple replied, "O Guruji! we should settle here permanently. This city is heaven on earth. Here the price of anything and everything is uniformly "one pice per seer". Anything under the sun that you require, from a pin or needle to silk and velvet or gold and gems, cost but one pice per seer. For a few annas we both can live the luxurious lives of kings. Let us remain here till the end of our lives."

No sooner the Guru heard this than he at once rolled up his deer-skin, tucked up his loin-cloth and, taking his staff and bowl, came out of the rest-house on to the open road. Addressing his disciple he said, "Let us leave this sinister place at once, O disciple! This is not heaven. It is Satan's own city. Come, tarry not a moment longer in this city of darkness. Each single second that you delay will endanger your very life. Where everything is almost free for the mere asking there life has verily turned topsy-turvy. Pleasure here will soon turn to dire danger and your smiles will give place to bitter tears. Come, let us leave this place at once."

The smile disappeared from the disciple's face. He became vexed and disappointed at the prospect of missing this feast of indulgence offered by the "pice-per-seer" commodities of Andhernagari. His rosy dream-palaces were coming trembling to the ground. He pleaded with the Guru to remain, urging him that nothing but joy would result from such a happy life, getting all things for a mere song and enjoying without much trouble or exertion. The Guru was earnest, serious and adamant. The disciple saw this and suddenly decided to break off from the Guru and remain in this paradise of milk and curd, fruits and sweets. Where else could one ever hope to get such a chance!

Thus he thought within his foolish self and told the Guru, "All right, if thou wilt go, go! I choose to remain in this city though you don't."

"Be it so," the Guru replied and, with a final warning, left the disciple and the city.

Thus the wayward disciple came to settle down in Andhernagari, the "City of Benightedness", where everything could be had for the mere asking, as it were. So cheap were things that an anna a day would suffice for a man to eat, drink and live in royal style. The disciple's life was one round of daily joy. He could eat to his heart's content. He could easily get whatever things desire dictated, and procure all that his senses craved for. Thus the five senses and the mind had their sense-demands satisfied even before they could arise. He had only to collect a few annas, which he easily did within half an hour by wandering into the well-to-do locality each morning. He gorged himself with tasty delicacies, regaled himself with fine perfumes and an occasional flower garland. His lips were ever crimson with the juice of fragrantly-spiced betel leaves and nuts. He looked quite distinguished in a silken gown and a smart orange-coloured turban. In the room which he came to occupy at the rest-house, there was

3

a fine cot (cheap at two annas, including cartage), with a soft bedstead upon it. A fine "hukka" with polished, silver decorative bands stood upon a stool made of carved ebony. There was a nice carpet on the floor too.

Thus passed five years. The disciple had the doorway widened somewhat since he first came to this room with his Guru. Good living had made him put on considerable flesh and he was now quite thick-set and bulky. He forgot his Guru, he forgot what he was and was only engrossed in enjoying the maximum of pleasures in this wonderful city, where he could get anything he wanted or wished for. Thus days, months and years passed on smoothly in a stream of ease and enjoyment. He eventually grew fat, gross, lethargic and sensual.

While the disciple lived thus, things in this great, topsy-turvy city went on as usual in their mad way. The minister of the country was a fool of the highest order. He was excelled only by his master, the king. The law of the land was of an extraordinary brand. The judges and law-givers vied with the king and the minister.

In this wonderful city there one day occurred an accident. A man was passing along a narrow roadway by the side of a newly constructed wall. As he was passing, the wall collapsed and a portion of it fell upon the man and injured him. He at once lodged a complaint to the magistrate against the owner of the wall. The day happened to be a Friday and it was the practice of the king to hold open court on all Fridays after 10 a.m. So cases occurring between 10 a.m. and 1 p.m. were taken directly before the king. Thus the injured man's complaint was referred to the open court, directly before the king. The trembling owner of the house was immediately hauled up before him.

His Majesty: "Now then, the wall belongs to you?"

Owner: "Yes, my king."

King: "Come, what have you to say? Why should you not be punished for the injury suffered by this man?"

Owner: "O Sarkar! though I own it, I know nothing about the wall. It was built entirely by a contractor who alone is responsible for its standing or its falling."

"Catch hold of the contractor and get him here at once!" roared the king.

The guards were at once despatched and soon the wretched contractor was brought before the court.

"Man!" thundered His Majesty.

The minister smiled in approbation.

King: "Your wall fell and injured one of my subjects. What have you to say now before I send you to the gallows?"

Contractor: "Doubtless I contracted the deal, my great king. But I pledge that it was the mason who really built the entire wall. He did the whole job. If he did it well, all would have been well. He did it ill and hence it fell and caused injury."

The king was pleased with the contractor. He vigorously shook his head up and down and said, "Yes, yes, you are right, my man. Go to the royal kitchen and have a drink of buttermilk."

Turning to the guards: "Go at once, hunt out and fetch me the mason."

The guards found the mason repairing a broken bridge. They swooped upon him suddenly and without the slightest warning caught him by the scruff of his neck and hurried him into the court.

"Speak for yourself before I hang you by the neck," roared the king in a terrible voice, "Vile mason, slayer of my subjects (here the king showered a tear and blew his nose), builder of tottering walls! How dare you commit such an atrocity?"

The mason gulped and rubbed his throat with his left hand. He was an elderly man with grey hair. He knew he was in a very bad situation, but luckily he had heard of the king's wisdom. He said, "Your Majesty, the fault is not mine. The mortar that went into the wall was not properly mixed and thus the work of the wall was not satisfactory."

"Who is the mortar mixer?" asked the king in an ominous tone.

The mason heaved a sigh of relief. He made haste to reply, "O my wise king! the mortar-mixer was a man called Buddhu Singh Gadbadi."

Now the court guards were getting wiser and knew what was coming next. So, before the king could turn to them, they were off and after a feverish search located Buddhu Singh, who was at that time partially drunk. Drunk or not drunk, the king wanted him and so the guards hauled him from his bottle to the court. Buddhu Singh wanted to shake hands with the king and the ministers. The guards had a hard time to make him understand that this was not done. Buddhu Singh could not see any sense in it. Ultimately, one of the guards had to administer a clout on his head. This sobered him a little.

"Why did you not mix the mortar well?" asked the king in a stern voice.

Buddhu Singh stared for a while, then blinked and replied, "What mortar?"

The minister intervened and said, pointing to the mason, "The mortar which you mixed for mason Akkal-lal."

6

Buddhu Singh was startled when he heard the mason's name. He seemed to have recollected something. He looked at the mason steadily and then howled out, "Huzur Sarkar, this man owes me two rupees and a half. He asked for it and I lent it. He borrowed it and has never returned it."

"Fool!" roared the king. "Do not talk of your money matters. Tell me about the mortar."

Buddhu Singh found himself where he was. He asked, "What mortar?"

Now the court was where it started. When the whole matter was explained with date, place, time and other particulars to the tipsy man, it at last entered his befuddled brain and he said, "Sarkar, In the name of my grandmother tell me how on earth I could mix my mortar properly when the rascal who was to supply me with water from the nearby tap across the street was the most atrocious idiot. He delayed and dallied for I know not why; never did he in time the water supply. Thus the mixture was either too wet or too dry or not ready when the mason wanted it."

The king was getting angry. The court was getting late. His dinner was delayed and yet the man to be hung did not seem easy to hit upon. Everyone seemed to have a perfect case, but justice must be done and a vigorous hunt was made for the water conveyor. His name was Macku Plastri and he lived in the outskirts of the town. He was very fond of music and he played upon a country-made flute. When he was caught, he was watering his garden with a leather bag. So he came to the court with the bag hanging by his side, dripping water.

"Take him to the gallows!" shouted the king.

The minister applauded. But the next moment the

king said, "Wait a minute. Let us ask the criminal a question. Why did you dally and delay water and foul the mortar mixture of Buddhu Singh?"

Macku Plastri replied, "I am not to blame, O great king! I had to get the water from across the street and as I was getting it, a dancing girl was singing a beautiful tune from her balcony. I am fond of music, so I stopped to listen. My leather bag is very leaky and as I listened to the song of the prostitute, all the water leaked out of the bag. If the prostitute did not sing from her balcony, I would have been prompt and proper in my duty."

"Release the man!" ordered the king. "Go and get the prostitute."

And thus it happened that as the prostitute was in her dressing room platting her hair, the guards summoned her to the court.

"Wretched woman," the king asked, "why do you sing from your balcony?"

The prostitute was frightened out of her wits and could think of no proper answer to the query. She was forthwith ordered to be executed and the guards hurried her to the gallows. Its work done, the court rose.

The courtesan now stood on the gallows. The hangman's noose was lowered over her head. The unfortunate woman was half dead with terror. But an extraordinary situation now cropped up. The lady was slender and thin. The hangman's noose was too big. It was many times oversize for her slender and small neck. Consternation prevailed. All the officials at the gallows were perturbed. How to do the hanging now? This was the question that agitated their minds. A man was sent post-haste to the minister. The minister was at his bath. He slided from the bathroom, wrapped up in a Turkish towel, and placed the matter before the king, who was at his dinner. The king was just eating an "imirthi" at the moment. He flourished his right royal gesture and ordered the minister: "Go! Convey my command at once that if this woman's neck is too small for the hanging noose, let them find a person of proper size to fit it and then do the hanging."

The minister withdrew. The king turned to the queen. She was a fat lady with very big teeth and had a great liking for butter and sweets.

"Look, my dear, all my subjects, from bottom to top, are perfect fools!" the king said, and continued to attend to the "imirthi".

The king's order was conveyed to the group at the gallows. They at once released the prostitute and told her to run away home after warning her about singing from the balcony.

Guards were at once sent to look for a man of sizeable proportions to fit the noose. Two of them happened to pass by the rest-house where the disciple was put up. The disciple had just had a very sumptuous dinner and was sitting leisurely in the open verandah in the sunlight, picking his teeth. His eyes had a far-away look, for he was contemplating upon what he would have for supper. He was also musing over the necessity of a comfortable nap just then. The guards espied him. Here was their man, well-fed, sleek and with a fat enough neck to take on the noose to a nicety. With an exultant "hurrah!" they rushed upon him and unceremoniously dragged him from the verandah to the street and hurried him along. The disciple loudly protested, remonstrated and pleaded, but to no avail. He was taken up and deposited on the gallows. Thoroughly frightened, he asked what they wanted to do with him.

The magistrate on the spot replied, "You have got to be hanged."

Disciple: "Why? I have done nothing."

Magistrate: "But what is it to us? The man was injured and the culprit is to be hanged."

"But I am not the culprit," cried the disciple.

"But then you are of the proper size. She was too small for the noose. As you fit it perfectly, up you go! You have got to dangle."

And the court poet, who was also the part-time court jester, said:

"Be you the culprit or be you no,
To join the majority you've got to go;
However much you may harangue and wrangle,
It is finally settled that you have got to dangle."

They then placed the noose around the fat neck of the disciple.

Now it was that the disciple remembered his good Guru's grave and serious warning: "O disciple! this is Satan's own city. Pleasure here will soon turn to dire danger and thy smiles will give place to bitter tears."

He now wept bitterly. He trembled in terror and sweat broke upon his forehead and flowed down his neck. He was in agony and cried: "O master, save me! Oh! Why did I disobey you? Why did I eat and grow fat in this city of darkness? I forgot why I originally came and joined my Guru. I forgot that true discipleship meant obedience to the Guru and a life of self-control. The attraction of enjoyment made me disobey my Guru's good advice. I did not heed his warning. I forgot my duty of renunciation, abstinence and self-control. I succumbed to the call of the senses and to the dictates of my pleasure-loving mind. I lived a life of excess and immoderation. I gave up my Sadhana. I did not do my duty. For the sake of my pleasure and self-will, I broke away from my Guru. Now this is the result. Retribution has overtaken me. O God! what am I to do?" Thus he lamented and wailed out bitterly.

Now there was a sudden stir in the crowd around the gallows. Someone pushed through to the front, crying out: "Stop! Stop!"

The hangman paused for a moment. A stately figure, a Sannyasin with matted locks, climbed onto the gallows and stood by the side of the disciple. It was the Guru. A man of intuition, he had suddenly come to know from far away that his erring disciple was in grave danger. So he immediately hurried post-haste to the city and arrived at the gallows at the critical moment.

The disciple now interrupted, saying, "No, no! Don't do it! Hang me! Be quick!"

But the Guru would not listen. He insisted upon taking the noose. The hangman was helpless. He looked at the magistrate and asked, "What is all this?"

But no one was listening to them, for the Guru and the disciple were engaged in a hot argument, each demanding that he be hanged, and refusing to give place to the other. This was a very extraordinary situation. It was beyond the magistrate's comprehension. Once again fresh messengers hurried to the king.

The matter was so extraordinary that the king himself now came in person. He demanded to know from the Guru why he wanted to hang himself. The Guru at first seemed unwilling to tell him, but when the king insisted, he said, "My dear king, there is a

11

very good reason for my wish. I am an expert and past master in Hindu astrology. I have come to know through my accurate calculation that there is an extraordinary, auspicious Muhurta at this time today, and that the person who dies during this Muhurta at this particular point of latitude and longitude where the gallows are situated and in this noose, that person will become the supreme emperor of this entire land in his immediate next birth. I want to become the emperor. Therefore, I have hurried with great haste to be in time at this spot. Well, you have the reason. Now let me be hanged quickly, before the Muhurta passes away!"

The king grew indignant. "Preposterous!" he cried. "You fellow! You to become the emperor? What audacity! What cheek! It is I who have to become the emperor. I shall be hanged now!"

So saying, Rajarajeshwar Brihat-moodh Bahadur slipped his head into the noose. There was great pandemonium. The Guru grasped the disciple by the hand and they both quickly hurried away from the spot and, walking fast, soon reached the outskirts of the city. The disciple was saved.

The disciple now fell in prostration before the Guru and clasped his feet. He accepted his error, expressed remorse and begged forgiveness from the Guru. The Guru lifted him up, blessed him and said, "Follow me."

Both turned their backs on the "City of Benightedness", the city of pleasures and plenty, and set out on the highway towards the Himalayas, where people lived in simplicity and self-control. They reached the little hamlet of saints on the banks of the Ganges, where the disciple lived an austere life of simplicity,

12

self-control, Sadhana, service of his Guru, obedience and devotion to God. He soon realised the Lord through the Grace of his Guru and obtained that bliss everlasting which is a million-fold more than all the sense-pleasures of the entire universe put together. He followed his Guru and from darkness came into light.

2

THE LOAD OF SINS

PARVATI WAS very proud. She thought that she had
never committed even one sin. She was sure that she
would be taken to heaven on her death in this world.

One morning she was sweeping the floor of her
house. By pure accident the broom fell on a cockroach
and it died instantly.

Parvati was greatly upset. She nearly went mad.
"Who will take this sin? How can I wash away this sin?
So far I have not committed even one sin. Now I have
done this. What am I to do?"

She ran here and there with the cockroach in her
hand. She was wonderstruck to see in the bazaar a
fish-vendor named Savitri.

Parvati asked her, "O wretched woman! what will
become of you when you die? You are daily killing so
many creatures. I have not committed even one sin till
this morning. Only today I accidentally killed this
cockroach, and even this sin I am struggling to wash
off by some mortification."

"Is that so?" asked Savitri. "Don't be very anxious. I
have killed millions of fish. You have not committed
any sin. This cockroach-sin need not worry you. Give
it here. I will add it to this basketful of fish-sin. You will

14

be freed instantly. You need not worry, and I won't either; the addition of a little cockroach to the basketful of fish is not going to make any difference."

Parvati was highly pleased. She gave away the dead cockroach to Savitri, who placed it in the basket of fish. Parvati was thoroughly relieved. Savitri was not concerned at all by her action.

It so happened that both women died on the same day. A heavenly chariot came to take Savitri to heaven, while the messengers of hell approached Parvati. Parvati was puzzled and enraged. She asked the messengers, "What! You must have made a mistake. I am not Savitri, the sinner. I am Parvati, the pious. Take Savitri and send the chariot for me to go to heaven."

"Good lady!" replied the messengers of hell, "we make no mistakes. You are wanted in hell. Savitri will go to heaven."

"But why?"

"O Parvati! it was the duty of Savitri to sell fish. She did not kill them for her pleasure but as a duty. She was devoted to her duty and at the same time she was devoted to God and did all her actions as offerings to the Lord and as His instrument. Therefore she merits heaven. You, on the other hand, killed a cockroach and felt 'I have killed a cockroach'. You did some charity and good actions only to fatten your egoism and pride. In your pride you thought disparagingly of saints and pious people. You never thought of God at all. You were haughty. You were extremely selfish. You even went to the extent of trying to transfer your sin to Savitri. She, on the contrary, was selfless enough to accept even that and to relieve you of the misery of sin-consciousness. Therefore she deserves to go to heaven and you to hell. Come, delay not."

15

3

THE AHIMSA-IDEAL

A POVERTY-STRICKEN man was walking through a grove. He was very hungry. He had not taken any food for the previous three days. The grove was full of mango trees and it was the mango season. The luscious fruit was too tempting, so the hungry man instinctively walked over to a stone, took it and threw it at the tree. A couple of mangoes fell on the ground. The man's face glowed with joy, and as his hands hungrily sought the fruit, his mouth dripped with saliva.

In the joy of having obtained the fruit to appease his hunger, the poor man did not give a thought to the course the stone had taken after cutting the fruit away from the tree. Having achieved its object, the stone had to fall. The momentum given by the man's hunger was great and the stone soared into the sky before dropping down.

Destiny, the creatrix of strange situations, had conspired to bring into that grove that day the poorest of men as well as the ruling monarch of the land. The poor man, at the threshold of death, sought something—anything—to appease his hunger. The great monarch, after a royal dinner, sought the cool shade of

16

the trees to while away his time by playing chess with his consorts and ministers. The monarch and the miserable wretch were unaware of each other.

The missile that struck the tree and felled the fruit was an inert stone; it couldn't respectfully avoid the monarch. It landed on his head. The turban protected the scalp, but it was thrown off and put out of shape. The monarch, immersed in delightful play with his consorts, had no mind to investigate the cause of the sad fate of the turban. But his courtiers could not brook the insult to the king. They sought the miscreant, the poor man who was greedily eating the luscious fruit.

The servants were eager to forestall the monarch's worst punishment and wanted to demonstrate their loyalty to him by meeting out capital punishment on one who had least offended his person. It happened in this case too that the king's ministers of law held an immediate court and on the spot condemned the poor man to death for assaulting the king.

The king rose from the game and the minister of law then announced that the miscreant had been severely punished for his outrageous act.

"Bring him to us," said His Majesty.

The poor man was brought before the monarch.

"Why did you throw the stone?"

"To obtain a mango."

"At what did you throw the stone?"

"At the tree."

"Did you get the mango?"

"Yes, Your Majesty."

"Have you eaten the mango?"

"Yes, Your Majesty."

The king turned to his minister of law.

"The poor man was hungry and he struck the tree with a stone. He obtained a mango and has eaten it. Now tell me, how long would he be free from hunger?"

"For about twenty-four hours, Your Majesty."

"That will do. Now we will pronounce our judgment."

The entire crowd waited with bated breath. Could it be something worse than the judge's sentence?

"We command that from today till the end of his life on earth this poor man shall receive from our treasury, wealth enough to maintain himself. Communicate this order at once to the finance minister."

Everyone was amazed! What manner of punishment is this?

The queen thought that she was responsible for it and that the pleasant mood that she had brought on in the king had put him in a light vein and so he had rewarded the poor man. She smiled significantly.

"My dear," said the king to the queen, "tell me, is the tree a sentient or an insentient object?"

"Of course, insentient, my lord."

"And I?"

"What a question to ask, great one! Man, the crown of creation, is a sentient being. You are a jewel among men. You are divinity truly. Who has surpassed thee in knowledge and wisdom?"

"Then, my beloved, is it not fair that I, a sentient being, prove that I am worthier than an insentient tree of this status that God has granted me?"

"You are, my lord; you are worthier than all men in fact and wisdom. But why do you say all this?"

"Look! The poor man struck the tree with a stone. It gave him a luscious fruit to eat. It appeased his hunger for a day. The stone fell on me as he threw it. It was

18

adjudged that he hit me with it. Should I not prove I am worthier than the tree? That is why I have ordered that his necessities be provided for throughout his lifetime."

The ministers, servants and the queen fell at the monarch's feet and kissed the dust beneath them. They glorified him.

"Our sovereign, you are truly Divinity upon this earth. Who but God Himself could manifest such compassion at a time like this! Lord! you rank in this virtue with Lord Buddha and Lord Jesus, with the great saints and sages of all times. Hail! Hail! May Your Majesty's wise and fruitful reign last for many years upon this earth. For, only rulers like you can inspire people to cultivate compassion, cosmic love and forbearance. Inspired by your glorious example, people will love each other, serve each other and thus purified at heart, will transform themselves into divine beings. Bless us, O lord, that we may be worthy servants of thee!"

4

RUNNING AWAY FROM EVIL

THROUGH PERSISTENT effort a sinner can become a saint. If you fly from evil, it will cling to you all the more.

In a certain highland, where stealing sheep was deeply resented and considered a crime, two brothers were caught in this nefarious act. To perpetuate the punishment, the village elders branded on their foreheads the letters "S.T". It signified "Sheep Thief". Then they were set free.

Both the brothers were extremely unhappy as the entire village came to know of the story; and whenever they were seen in public the people jeered at them, and the children were hilarious at their wake.

"There goes the S.T! Look out for the sheep thief!" they would cry out.

The elder brother took the ignominy seriously and thought to himself: "Let me run away from it all." He left the village and wandered through hills and dales, but alas! nowhere could he find peace. The staring trademark on his forehead attracted attention wherever he went and he was pestered with many questions.

"What do the letters mean? Who branded those

letters on your forehead?" For some time he tried to evade these inevitable enquiries. But how long could he succeed? Now and then he had to change from place to place. He grew more and more restless day by day, and finally died of bitterness and frustration. He was buried in lonely soil, away from the warmth of his home.

But the younger brother decided to stay on where he was. "There can be no running away from the fact of my crime," he thought, and bore the public insult with a stout heart. He had decided to forget the past and to open a new chapter in his life. With undaunted zeal, through months and years, he gradually built up a very high reputation for honesty and integrity. To his neighbours he became a symbol of goodness and virtue. His sore was healed by the cosmic healer—time—and people forgot about his past in due course.

Years later, some stranger came to the village and found the old man with the letters "S.T." branded on his forehead. He enquired from a neighbour what they meant.

"It is an old, old story," said the neighbour. "I do not remember the particulars, but they must be an abbreviation of 'saint'."

The moral of the story is that through persistent effort a sinner can certainly become a saint. No one can indeed fly from evils or wrongs of his actions. They follow him like shadows. The more he thinks of his past, the more his conscience is haunted. His mind clings to him wherever he goes.

Few are born saints. The story illustrates the fact that a sinner of today is a saint of tomorrow. Through sincere effort and a determination to succeed, even the most vicious nature can be turned into a saintly one. The transformation of rogue Ratnakar into sage Valmiki is an epic example of this truth.

Therefore, O Ram! do not be down-hearted because of your shortcomings. However heinous may your past be, through an unflinching will you can certainly overcome your defects and become a shining example of virtue and ethics to all those around you. Cheer up! Start your Sadhana right now.

5

THE LORD'S COMPASSION

NARAYANA PRASAD'S mother had passed away. Contrary to expectations, Narayana Prasad was extremely happy! He ran to his worship room, fell prostrate at the feet of his Deity—Jaganatha—and prayed: "Unasked you showered your Grace upon me. You have removed the one tie that bound me to this earthly life. I shall now be able to devote my entire life to you and you alone, without any distractions. Lord, grant me pure devotion."

Narayana Prasad and his mother had both been great devotees of Lord Jaganatha of Puri. Narayana Prasad now wended his way to Puri. All along the way he was singing the Names of the Lord in blissful self-forgetfulness.

In the heart of the devotee dwelt the Lord. Narayana Prasad communed with Him uninterruptedly. He did not think of going into the temple of Jaganatha of Puri. Instead, he went to the seashore and engaged himself in ceaseless repetition of His Name and meditation on His glories.

Three days passed. Narayana Prasad had not taken any food nor did he think of it. He was in a remote place; no pilgrims passed that way. He was starving, but immersed in the bliss of Kirtan and meditation.

23

Lord Jaganatha turned to His consort: "Lakshmi, what a pity! My devotee is starving on the seashore. I have neglected My duty; I have been heartless and cruel. He has been intent on the performance of his duty—remembrance of Me. But I have failed in Mine— the protection of the devotee. How can I face him now? I am burning with shame. You kindly go to him with delicious food and offer it to him."

Lakshmi agreed. She took on a golden plate the richest articles of the Lord's *prasad.*

Narayana Prasad was oblivious of the world. He was immersed in the Lord's Name. Lakshmi, while approaching him, felt shy to meet him face to face. She too felt unhappy at the thought that a devotee had thus been allowed to starve by the Lord and Herself. Quietly She placed the gold plate behind Narayana Prasad and swiftly returned to Her abode.

Narayana Prasad heard the sound of anklets; he turned his head towards the direction from which the sound came. He saw the gold plate of food but could not see anyone who could have brought it to him. He felt hungry. He thanked God for the timely shower of Grace and ate the food with great relish, as His *prasad.* Three nights of sleeplessness induced him to fall into slumber after the meal.

He awoke to find four stout Brahmins armed with batons standing around him.

"You wretched thief!" they cried, "how dare you steal the gold plate from the *sanctum sanctorum* of the Lord! Come! Get up! you vilest wretch. Follow us to the Rajah's palace and receive your punishment at his hands."

Narayana Prasad was perplexed at first. "I have not stolen this plate," he thought, "but why couldn't the person who brought the food for me on this plate take it back?" Instantly he composed himself and felt that it was useless to waste his thoughts over what was happening and instead went on with his mental Bhajan.

The king was greatly enraged. He ordered whipping of the culprit. The heartless servants of the king were overjoyed at this opportunity of giving vent to their power and glory. The whip fell on Narayana Prasad with ever-increasing force. The king's servants felt amazed at the sight. The devotee was laughing and singing His Names. After half an hour of whipping, they could not discover any mark of the whip on his body! They gave it up as useless and drove him out of the palace.

Narayana Prasad returned to his seashore residence and was lost in the thought of the Lord. Food arrived at night, but this time the plate was mysteriously taken away after he had eaten.

The Rajah could not sleep that night. He was haunted by a nightmarish feeling that he was being thrown out of his bed. Now and again he saw the image of Lord Jaganatha appear before him, and he saw blood was oozing from His waist. The Rajah was perplexed. He got up, ran out and reached the temple. He asked the priests to open it at once so that he could have the Darshan of the Lord.

The priests and the king were speechless when they discovered a stream of blood trickling from the Lord's waist and running into the *sanctum sanctorum*. The Rajah understood. His heart burned with sorrow, remorse and wretchedness at his crime. He understood in an instant that this strange happening was due to his thrashing of the poor Bhakta that afternoon.

25

Accompanied by his servants, the Rajah ran to the seashore; he fell prostrate at Narayana Prasad's feet. He begged pardon for his folly and pleaded for the healing of the wound on the Lord's body which Narayana Prasad alone could do.

Narayana Prasad wept bitterly. "My Lord! O ocean of mercy! What a thing for you to do! Why should you endure this torture for the sake of your poor devotee? Why could you not have prevented the Rajah's servants from whipping me instead of taking on cruel punishment on Thy own body?" He cried aloud in anguish. The blood-trickling ceased.

The Lord answered His devotee: "Narayana Prasad! know that according to your Prarabdha, you had to undergo this punishment. Such was your love for Me, such was your devotion to Me, that you had completely surrendered yourself to Me. It was My duty to protect you from all injury. Yet, I could not nullify your Prarabdha Karma, it had to be worked out. I had therefore to receive on My own body the whipping which was the preordained lot of your body. The Bhakta gets what is preordained according to his Prarabdha, but he is not affected by it. He does not suffer on account of it because I throw My protecting arms around him."

In the blazing Light of the Lord, Narayana Prasad disappeared!

26

6

THE PIGEON IN PRISON

THE RAJAH OF TANJORE was on his death-bed. Doctors had given up hope. The grief-stricken members of the royal household hung their long faces and awaited the end of the life they loved. Sleepless nights and torrents of tears had left them weary and speechless; their blank looks sought the floor more than the face of the monarch.

"Get thee gone, you beggar! Great doctors have failed. Are you going to succeed?" shouted the gate-keepers of the royal household. The target was a mendicant. Little did they realise that he was the renowned saint Raghaviah.

Raghaviah was a contemporary of the great Muslim Mahatma, who has since been known by the name of Nagore Andavan. They lived the lives of Avadhootas. Their almost naked bodies clung "loosely" to their enlightened souls, which were ready to fly away to their original sweet home at any moment. Their calm, bearded faces radiated a peace that captivated all. The light in their eyes put to shame the most ravishing beauty of human form. There was something about them that compelled attention, reverence and love.

Raghaviah and Nagore Andavan were one at heart.

27

Many were the miracles they played together. In all cases they aimed at the good of all. They healed the sick, brought prosperity to the faithful and conferred spiritual felicity on the devout.

Raghaviah gazed at the care-worn faces of the gate-keepers. "May not a beggar succeed where doctors have failed? Tell me what the matter is with the king. Let me see if I can help. I am not here to beg but to bless."

The elderly mother of the Rajah heard this calm, stout-hearted declaration of the monk. The maternal heart clung to a ray of hope that this apparently insignificant person gave her. She ran to greet the beggar. The gatekeepers looked away in perfect disdain. A drowning man clutches even at the floating straw.

"May I see the Rajah, mother? Perhaps God might show us some way out."

Struggling between hope generated by the Sadhu's confidence and hopelessness betrayed by his appearance, the mother took him to the Rajah's room.

Raghaviah gazed at the Rajah in silence. He smiled. In spite of themselves, all those around him smiled; they felt their burden lighten.

"I cannot prescribe any medicine myself," said Raghaviah.

The women burst into tears.

"But I can tell you where to find relief."

Between sobs, the mother pleaded, "Please!"

"Go at once to Nagore Andavan. You will find him underneath a tree in the mangrove. Represent your case to him. He will give you the necessary medicine to cure the Rajah."

A party sped along the road to Nagore. The royal

mother's heart was a mile in advance! The most venerable but usually haughty mother of the Hindu monarch lay prostrate at the feet of the half-naked, ash-besmeared body of the Muslim Fakir, Nagore Andavan.

"Save my son, Prabho!" cried the mother, catching hold of the feet of the Fakir.

The Fakir turned his head away.

"Huh! You do all sorts of foolish things and then come to me when you are in danger. All right, will you do just as I tell you to do?"

"Yes, Prabho, anything."

"Go straight to the palace. Near the ceiling above the king's head you will find a newly-plastered circle on the roof. Cut it open. A pigeon is struggling for its life in the wall. Release it forthwith. Your son will be all right. It is on account of this heartless action of his that he is suffering. Exactly the same pain that afflicts the pigeon the king has to endure. If the pigeon breathes its last, the king too will die at the same moment. Rush! He will survive, but you must take a vow this very moment never to cause the least injury to any living creature. Remember that all life is sacred. An ant has as much right to lead its own life as the highest Brahma has. Man has no business to interfere with the life-course of any being. Go!"

The mother rushed to the palace armed with the saint's blessings. She made straight for the Rajah's chamber. Masons were summoned and the plaster was removed in an instant. It was a pitiable sight. Struggling between life and death lay a pigeon, its half-closed eyes reflecting the voiceless agony it was enduring within the lethal chamber. The mother nursed it back to recovery. The Rajah sat up in his bed.

Every grain of rice that the pigeon ate, every drop of water that was put into its mouth revived the Rajah.

The Rajah admitted: "There was a hole in the wall over my bed. Pigeons used to live in it. They soiled my bed. I felt they were a nuisance, so I ordered that the hole be blocked."

The mother was impatient. "You have been saved, son, by the miraculous Grace of Fakir Nagore. Go to him. Bow to him. Take the vow in his presence that you will never cause the least pain to any living being. Lose no time."

The Hindu monarch's crown swept the dust of the Muslim Fakir's feet. It was he who originated the name "Nagore Andavan", by which the saint has since been known.

The Rajah had a huge temple built on the Samadhi of the saint after the latter had passed away. He gave vast lands to the temple and willed that thousands of pigeons be fed from the produce of those lands. This custom is adhered to till today, and the temple continues to radiate miraculous Grace, healing power, peace, unity and prosperity.

Glory to Nagore Andavan! My salutations to him!

7

MAN—THE GLORY OF CREATION

THE CUNNING FOX was vexed at the glorification of man and his exalted position in God's creation. It thought within itself: "Am I in any way less intelligent than man? Or is he less cunning than I am when he wants to cheat others? He is a living creature just as much as I am. In fact I am more contented than he. I don't wear costly or a variety of clothes every season. I endure heat and cold patiently. I do not ask for umbrellas to protect me from the rain, or dark glasses to prevent the glare of the sunlight in summer. I do not ask for a motor-car or train to go from place to place. Though we animals possess all these and many more noble qualities, why should man be considered as superior to us. I shall see that this injustice is put to an end."

The fox ran hither and thither and incited other animals to join him. He was able to gather a number of them. Then they all went to the elephant. The wise elephant said, "Brothers, there is no doubt some truth in what you say. Let us then go to another forest dweller and ascertain his views. There lives a sage in yonder cottage. Let us go to him and represent our case."

They all agreed to the elephant's suggestion.

"Swami, you know me well," barked the dog. "I am the symbol of gratitude. If a man beats me a thousand times and gives me a morsel of food but once, I am grateful to him throughout my life, and ready to give up my life in his service. But man forgets a thousand services rendered to him and remembers the one wrong that his friend might have done. Completely ignoring the help received, he is ready to murder his kith and kin if he is wronged once, even unwittingly. How then, Sir, can you say that man is superior to beasts?"

And this was the cow's plea: "Man takes me to the pastures to graze. Sometimes he gives me a little straw or husk. In return I give him my nourishing milk. Sometimes he even starves my baby in order to feed himself and his children. When I thus feed him and his family, he gives me shelter in a foul-smelling and unclean place at the backyard of his house. The moment I go dry, I am ill-treated and ignored. If I become old, I am driven out or sold to a butcher. Such is man whom you exalt sky-high. Please Sir, tell me why."

Now it was the crow's turn: "Has man got this one quality that I possess, Sir? Even if a small crumb of bread is thrown to me, I crow and call all my brothers and sisters to share it with them. But man does just the opposite. However much he has, he hoards still more and even goes out of his way to snatch the bread of his neighbour. How can this selfish and greedy man be exalted above me?"

The fish whispered: "O sage! I shall not call man inferior to me, but I call him downright foolish! I cause him no harm. In fact I serve him by keeping the ponds, tanks, lakes and rivers clean. I eat away the dirt that is thrown into the water by him. But instead of preserving such a good benefactor, this foolish man catches me and kills and eats me! Do you regard this foolish man superior to me?"

The mule brayed: "O Sir! the fish is quite right. Look at my pitiable plight. I am a beast of burden. I am famous for the divine quality of patience. I bear insult and injury patiently. Without my service, the people in the hills will perish for want of the necessities of life. I carry their food and other goods. What is my reward? Beating and more beating! Is this man superior to me?"

"Tell him everything, friends, tell him all about your qualities and your supernatural attainments," chimed in the cunning fox.

"Sir," said the deer, "the very skin on which you sit and meditate on God belongs to our kind. Have you ever heard of man's skin being put to any good use? In the matter of beauty, the most beautiful eyes of a damsel are often compared to mine. My lovely horns decorate man's halls."

"So also," said the peacock, "my feathers are so charming that even Lord Krishna had them tucked into His turban. Lord Shanmukha uses me as His Vahana, and many of His devotees and Mantravadis use my feathers as magic wands to drive off evil spirits. No one has ever heard of man's skin or hair being so used."

"All my excretions have been considered holy and highly purificatory," said the cow. "The Panchagavya is an invariable item in all the holy rites of man. The very mention of human excretions will induce only vomiting in man and the least contact with them has

33

to be followed by a thorough wash and bath."

"Can any man boast of having such a wonderful sense of smell as I have?" enquired the dog.

"Can any man boast of having such a wonderful sense of sight as I have?" asked the kite.

"Can any man see during the night and the day with equal ease as I can?" asked the cat.

"I can do great things, Sir. I have an enormous body. There are numberless stories of my intelligence. My tusk and bones are converted into lovely ivory images and idols. All this is true, Sir. But kindly enlighten us as to why man is considered superior to us. Though I do agree with the arguments of my brothers, I feel that there must be some wise reason for this."

All the animals waited patiently to listen to the sage.

The sage said, "Listen, my kinsmen of the jungle! All that you have said is true. But God has endowed man with a sixth sense, the eye of discrimination, the Buddhi which distinguishes the right from the wrong, the truth from the untruth, the good from the evil. You are governed by instinct. Man can attain intuition. He can control his instincts and through intuition attain God."

"And if he doesn't?" asked the cunning fox.

"If he doesn't, he is of course worse than a beast. If he does, he is far superior to all else in creation," said the sage.

The animals went away satisfied.

34

8

THE GURU'S LOVE

"MASTER, HOWEVER MUCH I try to restrain it, my mind wanders towards the enjoyments of this world. Often I think of leaving you without informing you. But my love for your lotus feet prevents me from taking such an ungrateful step. My Lord, what must I do? Please guide me," Ram thus pleaded to his Guru, Premananda. It was just a month since he had entered the Ashram of his Guru.

"Child, I too have been watching your keen, inner struggle. Deeply embedded desires are hard to conquer. Fear not. Go forth into the world. Lead the life of a householder for some time and satisfy the intense craving of your mind. But all the time fix your mind on the Lotus Feet of the Lord. Never lose sight of your goal. Come back after ten years. Do not stay longer.

Ram took leave of his Guru. He went to his home town, married and settled down to family life. He had served his Guru with heart and soul, and had earned his Guru's Grace. Success waited upon him. Soon he was one of the most prosperous men in the town, with a loving wife and lovely children.

Ten years rolled by.

A mendicant stood on the doorstep of Ram's bungalow. His children ran into the house in fright. Ram's wife was showering the vilest abuses on the Sadhu. The Sadhu remained unmoved and wanted to see the master of the house. Ram recognised his Guru. In a dignified manner he greeted his old master and offered him a seat.

"Well, Ram, ten years are over. Have you been able to satisfy yourself yet?"

"I have enjoyed all that the world has to offer, my Gurudev. I could have myself come away to rejoin the Ashram. But how can I leave these little children uncared for? Please allow me to stay for a few more years, educate them and see that they are settled in life. Then I shall surely join you."

Ten more years rolled by.

This time it was an aged decrepit Ram that greeted the Sadhu. His wife had departed from the world. His sons were young men now with families of their own.

"My beloved Guru," Ram said, "it is true I have fulfilled my duties of a household life. All my children are now grown up and are prosperous in life. Yet they are young. They are immersed in the pleasures of the world. They have no sense of responsibility. Left to themselves, they might squander away all the hard-earned wealth of their father and then starve. I have to plan their family budget and guide their actions. Please allow me to remain here for a few more years till they grow up into full manhood and assume the responsibilities of the household. Then I shall certainly come away and join the Ashram."

Seven years rolled by after this.

The Sadhu, Premananda, returned to Ram's house to see his disciple.

36

The Guru's Love

A big dog was guarding the gate. He recognised it; it was Ram. He went into the house to learn that old Ram had passed away a couple of years back. Such was his attachment to the family that he took birth as a dog and guarded his house and his children. Premananda entered into the spirit of the dog.

"Well now, my child, are you ready to follow me?"

"Surely a couple of years hence, my Guru," replied the dog-Ram. "My children are now at the peak of their good fortune and prosperity but they have several jealous enemies. In a couple of years they will be free from fear and worry. Then I shall run to your Ashram."

Ten more years elapsed.

The Sadhu returned to Ram's house. The dog too had died. He saw through his intuitive vision that Ram had assumed the form of a venomous cobra and was guarding the iron safe in the house. Premananda made up his mind that the time had come to deliver his disciple from delusion.

"Brother," he spoke to Ram's grandson, "there is a venomous cobra in the cavity near the iron safe. It is a dangerous one. Kindly have it removed from there. Please do not kill it. Give it a good beating, break its back and bring it to me."

The young man was astonished to find that the Sadhu's words were true. He gathered all the youngsters of the household and began to belabour the cobra. As commanded by the Sadhu, they did not kill the cobra, but so injured it that it was unable to move. The Sadhu fondly caressed its head and then, throwing it around his own shoulders, quietly took leave of Ram's grandchildren. They too were extremely happy to be thus miraculously saved from the venomous cobra by the Sadhu.

On his way the Sadhu spoke to the cobra: "Beloved Ram! no one has so far been able to satisfy his senses and mind. Cravings are insatiable. Before one disappears a dozen others crop up. Discrimination is your only refuge. Wake up! At least in your next birth you should attain the Supreme."

"Gurudev!" Ram cried bitterly. "How gracious you are! Even though I proved ungrateful to you, you have always graciously followed me and, never losing sight of me, have guided me back to your lotus feet. Surely there is none in the whole world who could be so full of divine love as a Guru. There is no selfless love in the world except between a true Guru and his disciple."

9

KANCHA PRABHU

ONCE UPON A TIME there lived in a distant village near Allahabad, a Vaishya by the name of Kancha Prabhu. His parents belonged to Mysore and he went out of his home town in search of business, finally settling in Allahabad. He dealt in piece-goods. By the Will of God he became very rich. He was so rich that he did not know exactly how much wealth he had in his possession. He had no sons. He had only a wife to serve him.

Days passed by. Kancha Prabhu became old. In all his lifetime he had never given anything in charity to anyone. So one day his wife, Santipriya, told him that they should do some charity and visit Banares and other places of pilgrimage at least once in their lives.

Kancha Prabhu was reluctant to undertake any pilgrimage for fear of losing his train fare and the food and other expenses in connection with the pilgrimage. He said that they need not go anywhere on pilgrimage and that Prayag was itself the holiest of Tirthas. It was enough if they took their bath in the Triveni at Prayag. His wife agreed.

Kancha Prabhu did not take any money with him for the purpose of charity. He simply tied a few grains

Inspiring Stories

of gram in a cloth and started for his bath in the
Ganges. He wanted to go to a Ghat where no Pandas
were waiting. It was the Sankranti day and all the
Ghats were full. He was terribly afraid of the Pandas for
they would demand money as Dakshina. So he took a
roundabout route and reached the Murda Ghat where
all the dead bodies were burnt.

Lord Siva found out the motive of the Bania and,
assuming the form of a Panda, seated Himself in the
Ghat. The Bania was terrified to see a Panda even in
the burning Ghat.

The Panda came near and said, "O Sethji! today is an
auspicious day. Have Sankalpa before bathing."

The Bania said, "I have no money."

The Panda replied, "You can give me Dakshina later
on. But simply tell me what you will give."

The Bania told him that he would give him one pie.
The Panda, who was Lord Siva Himself, was pleased
and performed all the rituals.

The Bania took bath and returned home along with
his devout wife, who had been watching everything
with interest. She could not say a word about request-
ing him to give Dakshina to the Panda lest he should
get angry.

Some time passed and the Panda approached the
Bania for his Dakshina. Kancha Prabhu was inside the
house. His wife informed him of the arrival of the
Panda. Kancha Prabhu was awfully puzzled as to how
he could save the promised Dakshina of one pie. He
felt that his life would depart from his body if he gave
away the amount in charity. He told his wife to ask the
Panda to come some time later, and pretended to have
high fever.

As instructed, his wife told the Panda that her

40

husband was unwell and that he would not be able to see him. The Panda said that he would surely see the Sethji since he was not well. It was, he said, his duty to attend on him when he was sick.

Santipriya informed her husband that the Panda was bent upon seeing him and serving him while he was sick. Now Kancha Prabhu was in a fix. He thought of a plan. He asked his wife to inform the Panda that his fever being severe, he had suddenly expired and that the Panda could depart. It was useless to wait anymore.

Hearing this the Panda said, "O dear lady! to my great misfortune my friend is dead. Now I shall do his last rituals and then only leave this place."

The lady conveyed the message to her husband. Then the Bania replied, "Dear Santipriya, this Panda will not leave me. Please bring the coffin and take me to the burial ground."

In great sorrow the lady put the body of her husband in the coffin. He was all along pretending to be dead.

The funeral procession started and reached the burning Ghat. The Panda chanted the Mantras and the body of the Bania was about to be placed in the fire. At once the Bania yelled and jumped out of the coffin! Seeing this, the Lord in the form of the Panda, laughed heartily and revealed His real form. He asked the Bania to choose a boon as He was pleased with him.

The Bania said, "O Lord! please forgive me and exempt me from paying your Dakshina!"

The Lord said, "Be it so," and disappeared.

Mysterious is attachment. Mysterious is human nature. Instances of this description can be found even today. Those who are watchful can see clearly the

Inspiring Stories

folly of clinging to mundane things and suffering endless pains and miseries.

Can you take even a single pie from this world when your life departs? You have to leave behind everything, including the body which you love so much.

10

THE WISDOM OF GOD

NO CREATION IS without its purpose. Every divine act is directed towards ultimate good.

Acharya Sri Ahankar Keshari was a man of great erudition. His tongue was like a double-edged knife, with which he could slice into a thousand bits all his opponents while in debate. He could bring down thunder and lightning into his verbose extollation of the sovereign, in whose court he served as a royal tutor.

The king presented the Acharya with a large garden where various kinds of delicious fruits were ever ready to whet the savant's palate and keep his razor-sharp intellect free from the pinch of the monster called hunger. There were also flower beds of many kinds to inspire his soliloquies during the morning and evening walks.

It was a wintry day, a Sunday. After his lunch the Acharya decided to take a stroll out in the garden. As he walked past the various fruit-bearing trees, he mused over the creations of God.

"How large are the pumpkins spread all over the thatch, and yet so thin is the creeper! Fresh, scarlet apples, how delicious! Blessed indeed is the tree!"

43

Thus he went along his walk, musing over the different kinds of fruits and different hues of flowers.

"Here is a bench at last. How tired I am!" he muttered as he deposited himself on a bench placed under a huge, hoary banyan tree. Looking up, he beheld the mighty branches and the dense leaves of the huge tree spread over such a large area.

"What a shame!" the Acharya thought, "such a huge, stout tree, with such an abundance of leaves, yet what a shame! So puny are its fruits. How foolish God has been in creating such a tree with practically no yield at all, whereas yonder, across the fields, the shining grapes, the smiling apples, the tempting pomegranates and, least of all, such enormous pumpkins attached to so slender a creeper. None of them boasts of the size of their trees, but yet each of them yields so bountifully. But this banyan here, towering above my head like a vast canopy, with no edible fruit at all—this mighty banyan tree—what a disgrace! A very stupid creation indeed!"

Musing thus, the Acharya fell asleep. The afternoon breeze was pleasant, and with the ticking of time, the learned man heaved up and down in rhythmical grace.

"Tup!" A tiny banyan fruit landed sharply on the shiny head of the Acharya. He was rudely roused from his sleep.

"Oh! what an escape! A miraculous escape! How gracious indeed is God! How farsighted is His vision, His acumen and His judgment!" cried Sri Ahankar Keshari. "O Lord! Thou art all-wise. Had the banyan fruit been slightly bigger, my head would have been split into bits; it would have been the end of this corporeal existence."

44

The Wisdom of God

The learned man had a new vision. He returned home extremely grateful to God for sparing his life.

Foolish man hastily concludes his decisions about the various divine acts that confront him day after day. All indeed is for the best. Every divine act is directed towards the ultimate good. None of God's actions is without its own purpose. Aspirants should guard themselves from hasty decisions. They should cultivate a calm, serene mind and sharpen their acumen. The God of all mercy could never be unwise in any of His acts, which may for the present seem quite without purpose and untoward to your good. They are for your ultimate well-being only and certainly have the greatest purpose. Therefore, always avoid a hasty judgment.

11

AYAZ

AYAZ, A MERE slave, became the chief minister of Mahmud Ghazni. Mahmud Ghazni loved him intensely. This aroused the jealousy of the other ministers. They tried their best to make the emperor angry with Ayaz and send him away. All their efforts and tricks proved futile. Ghazni loved Ayaz all the more.

The ministers one day asked Mahmud Ghazni, "O adorable emperor! please tell us why you love this slave so much."

The emperor replied, "Yes, there is a positive reason for this. You will know after some time."

Some two months later the emperor called all his ministers, including Ayaz, and said, "My beloved ministers, tomorrow I will hide myself in the royal garden outside the city. Start looking for me early in the morning and find me before sunset. I will give rich presents to those who find me."

All the ministers gladly consented and went to their homes with cheerful hearts. Their minds were ever on the nature of the presents they would get the following day. They did not even get good sleep during the night.

Ayaz

That night the emperor ordered that all the streets leading to the city gates should be filled with groups of singers and dancing parties of young, beautiful damsels. Accordingly the dancers and singers filled the streets the next morning.

All the ministers started for the city gates at dawn. On their way, however, they could not resist the temptation of listening to the music and witnessing the dance performances of the young, beautiful girls. Every minister thought within himself, "The garden in which the emperor is hidden is a small one. I will be able to find him in a few minutes. Let me enjoy the music and the dance. I have not witnessed anything like this in my lifetime. All these girls are expert songsters and dancers."

The sun was about to set. The ministers started in a hurry to the gates to reach the garden outside. But by the time they reached the garden, the sun had already set. To their shame and dismay they found their emperor in the happy company of Ayaz.

The ministers asked Ayaz, "When did you come here? Did you not witness the dancing and singing parties?"

Ayaz said, "What dancing and singing parties? I did not see any. I came straight to the garden at sunrise and met my master. I have been with him all the time since then."

The emperor said, "Look here, my beloved ministers! that is the reason why I love Ayaz intensely. His eyes see nothing but me, his heart has no place for anything save myself. How can I forget him? How can I cease loving him? He is dearer to me than life itself. How can I ignore him?"

You must also love the Lord with such whole-

47

hearted devotion as Ayaz loved his master. Your eyes should see nothing but the Lord. Your heart must have no place for anything but your Beloved. You must ever chant and sing His Name and glories. Only then will He enthrone Himself in your heart. He will Himself become your lover. You will dwell in Him happily for ever.

12

LOVE ALONE CAN TRANSFORM

IN TIMES OF YORE, a small Ashram consisting of a few huts and a temple surrounded by a big garden of flowers, herbs and different kinds of plants and trees, was situated far from towns and cities on a hill-slope by the side of a swift-flowing stream adjoining the Oudh forest. A saint, along with his six disciples, lived there. He was a devotee of Lord Gopala and used to call himself His servant. Hence his name became Gopaldas and the Ashram was called Gopal Ashram.

Gopaldas was a saint and herbalist too, and famous for his nobleness, kindness, purity, loving behaviour and successful free treatment of all kinds of patients without any distinction of caste, creed or colour, rich or poor. He always kept open house, never demanding anything in lieu thereof. If any rich man of his own accord donated a sum of money, almost the whole amount was utilised in the preparation of medicines and lodging and feeding of poor patients and other visitors. But he and his disciples mostly lived on alms, which were generally collected in turn by two disciples going from door to door in nearby villages.

A young landlord, Jagdish Singh, was well known

for his cruelty and loose conduct. He was very much afraid of Gopaldas. He had a honeyed tongue and a heart of gall. He never liked Gopaldas but always pretended to respect him whenever they met. Many a time he sent sinful, mischievous and immoral persons to hurt and harm Gopaldas and his Ashram. A few of them returned, for they would not dare to approach the saint. Some went to the Ashram, but as soon as they saw Gopaldas, their minds were changed and they disclosed their intentions. Gopaldas always heard everything very calmly and kept quiet and smiling. The landlord, finding that all his efforts had failed and his intentions laid bare, made friends with one Karan Singh, a renowned dacoit and culprit living in the nearby forest with his gang. Both met, drank, dined together and made plans.

Gopaldas had a most handsome horse, which was not only very attractive, but belonged to a special and famous breed, scarcely available. It had all the qualities of a fine horse. It was very useful and dear to Gopaldas.

One day, while going to see a patient in a certain village, Gopaldas rode through the forest. Karan Singh saw him and decided to attack, but his courage gave way. However, on his way back, Karan Singh appeared on the road disguised as a lame beggar and began to sigh. When the saint saw him he was filled with love and compassion and made him sit on the horse while he himself started walking.

After covering some distance, the dacoit spurred on the horse, leaving the saint behind. He shouted in a loud voice, "O foolish Sadhu! I am Karan Singh. I decided to plunder your horse which I have done tactfully. Now you can't get it back."

50

Gopaldas laughed and replied, "The horse is well trained and will come back to me even now if I whistle. But I do not want to do that. I am glad to see that I am able to serve Gopal in thy form."

After a pause he continued, "Kindly do me a favour if possible."

Karan Singh enquired in a stern manner, "What favour do you expect from Karan Singh? Do not try to fool me."

Gopaldas replied, "Do not think in that manner. You can take the horse, but please do not tell anyone about this event."

"What harm will come to you in my doing so?" asked Karan Singh.

"After hearing about this event, people may not trust and help the poor and needy in future," said Gopaldas. And saying so, he returned to his Ashram.

His words, however, fascinated Karan Singh, who was ashamed of his act and behaviour. Throughout the night he remained restless and could not sleep a wink. The next morning, along with the horse, he went to Gopal Ashram, where he was received like a friend. He fell at the feet of Gopaldas and said beseechingly and with a heavy heart, "I have now decided to give up my profession entirely. I request thy forgiveness, shelter and kindness."

Gopaldas took him in his arms with love and replied, "Don't worry. Be calm. Probably you have not slept for the whole night. Therefore go to the *kutir* and take rest." At the same time he instructed one of his disciples to arrange for his lodging and food.

When the landlord came to know of this, he flushed with anger. Now, deciding to put the whole Ashram on fire himself, and to end the existence of Gopaldas

51

and Karan Singh, he started at midnight with his few trustworthy servants. Jagdish Singh, the landlord, was on the horse leading the party. As they reached the Ashram hill, he asked his men to extinguish all their torches except one. The party now began to ascend. When they were just near the Ashram, his horse suddenly slipped and, with a loud neigh, fell along with his master into a ditch. The dogs of the Ashram started barking. The servants were quite confused and terrified, being unable to decide what to do.

Soon they noticed a few persons coming towards them with burning torches in their hands. Just as they were intending to run away, they heard a sympathetic voice say, "Please do not be frightened. I am coming to help you."

Gopaldas, accompanied by his four disciples and Karan Singh, reached the spot and enquired about the matter. One of the servants revealed the truth. Karan Singh, on hearing it, was greatly agitated. Gopaldas at once went down with a torch in his hand, followed by his disciples and the landlord's servants. Karan Singh remained standing where he was. They found Jagdish Singh taking his last breath, half hanging on the branch of a tree in an unconscious state and badly injured.

Gopaldas carried him to his *kutir*, washed his wounds, applied medicines and bandaged him carefully. Then he put some liquid medicines into his mouth to bring him back to consciousness and sat at his side waiting for the result.

Karan Singh, who, throughout the episode had been looking on at everything with a strange look of hate mixed with anger, now said respectfully to Gopaldas, "Pardon me, Sir, your holiness had to suffer so many

52

times due solely to this wicked Jagdish, and even now your noble self is trying to bring him back to life with so much pain and care."

Gopaldas, motioning with his finger, requested him to remain quiet.

In the morning, when the sun was just beginning to peep from the gates of heaven, Jagdish Singh slowly opened his eyes. He looked around once and closed them again. Gopaldas prayed to Lord Gopala and silently thanked Him. Then he went out of the *kutir*, taking Karan Singh along with him.

"Hate produces hate, whereas love transforms hate into love. There is a vast difference between conquering others by the force of power and by the force of divine love," said Gopaldas.

He continued, "The two are opposed to each other. The former is like poison whereas the latter is like divine nectar and extends its benefits to both. While the one temporarily brings the enemy to one's knees, the other permanently subdues him for ever. Love is God and God is love. Love and love alone can transform."

Meanwhile, a disciple came running and intervened by informing that Jagdish Singh had opened his eyes again and he was probably searching for someone. Gopaldas rushed towards the *kutir* and both Karan Singh and the disciple followed. Jagdish Singh was not in a position to speak because his lower jaw was badly injured. Although his eyes were closed he heard the light sound of Gopaldas's footsteps coming in.

After a minute or so Jagdish Singh again opened his eyes, but his look was quite different to the previous one, for it appeared that his heart was burning and melting with the heat of his past actions. Shame and repentance—these same thoughts and feelings were rolling on his cheeks from both the eyes in the form of sorrowful tears, full of gratitude and obligation towards the saint, who was an embodiment of love and forgiveness.

Understanding Jagdish's thoughts and feelings, Gopaldas blessed and consoled him by putting his palm gently on his head.

13

LIVING PRESENCE OF GOD

DESPAIRED OF GETTING the coveted fruit of Sadhana, Puran Chand approached his Guru.

"Useless! Six months of worship of the idol of Narayana has produced no effect at all. Kindly suggest a more powerful Mantra and more powerful Deity."

The Guru had initiated Puran Chand into the Narayana Mantra and given him a small, beautiful idol of Lord Narayana for worship. Puran was regular in the worship, ceaseless in his Japa. God knows why, but there was no sign of the idol blessing him.

The Guru smiled at Puran. "Well son, take this idol of Lord Siva. I will presently initiate you into the Siva Mantra—the holy Panchakshara. Worship Lord Siva with faith and devotion. He is considered Bholenath. He is easily propitiable. He will bless you soon."

Puran Chand was overjoyed.

The next six months saw Puran Chand immersed in Japa and worship of Lord Siva. The idol of Narayana went on the dusty shelf above the altar in his worship room.

"No use in this either. Not a trace of effect. My Lord, please do not test me. Kindly give me initiation into the Mantra and the idol of that Deity who will soon bless me," Puran Chand pleaded with his Guru.

The Guru smiled again. The time for enlightenment had arrived, yet he felt that the disciple will learn for himself by experience.

"Good, my son. In this age, Mother Kali is most gracious. Worship this image of Hers. Repeat the Navarna Mantra. You will attain Her Grace very soon indeed."

This time Puran Chand had no misgiving whatsoever; he had full faith.

Kali worship commenced. Siva joined company with Lord Narayana on the shelf. With great devotion and feeling, Puran was waving incense before the image of Mother Kali. The fumes rose up. He watched. They reached the shelf too. He was enraged. He laid the incense down and got up.

"Well, what business has this Lord Siva, who refused to be propitiated and who refused to bless me, to inhale this incense? I am worshipping Mother Kali now. I will not allow this fragrant incense to enter Siva's nostrils. I will plug them with cotton."

Puran set about the task. He took the rusting idol of Siva in his hands and began inserting cotton into its nostrils!

Lo! The idol disappeared. In front of him stood the Lord, smiling in all His mercy and compassion. Puran was on his knees.

"Ask for any boon, Puran. I am greatly pleased with your devotion."

"My Lord, first tell me. I am perplexed. You did not deign to bless me when I devoutly worshipped you, when I repeated the Panchakshara Mantra for six months. But you suddenly chose to reveal yourself to me when I had discarded your image and given up your worship. What is this mystery?"

"My child, there is nothing mysterious in this. How could I reveal Myself when you treated Me as a mere image, as a mere piece of metal, to be worshipped and discarded at your sweet will or whim? But when you treated the idol as a living Presence, when you began to plug the nostrils with cotton so that the incense may not enter those nostrils, and thus revealed that you recognised my living Presence in that idol, I could no more withold Myself from you."

Speechless and enlightened, Puran bowed to Lord Siva and was immersed in His love. He could ask for no boon. In His love he found everything.

14

NARADA'S MUSIC PRIDE QUELLED

RISHI NARADA became proud of his skill in playing the *veena*. Lord Krishna wanted to remove this defect.

Once, many talented musicians were present at the Durbar of Lord Krishna. Hanuman and Narada were also there. Lord Krishna asked Narada to play the *veena*. Narada gave a delightful performance. Everyone appreciated the musical talent of the great Rishi, and all except the Lord began to shake their heads in ecstasy.

At the end of the performance, Lord Krishna asked Sri Hanuman, "O monkey chief! what do you think of the music of Narada?"

Narada Rishi took this as a great insult and hung his head in shame.

Lord Krishna enquired, "O Rishi! why do you look so dejected?"

Narada kept silent for a few minutes and then replied, "O adorable Lord! many talented musicians are present in this gathering. You have ridiculed me by asking a monkey, who does not understand even the rudiments of music for his opinion on my music. I am indeed very much afflicted at heart."

Lord Krishna said, "Dear Narada, do not be

offended. Please give your *veena* to the monkey-chief.
Let us find out whether he knows the art of playing or
not."

Narada became even more annoyed and began
muttering something.

Lord Krishna asked, "O Narada! what are you
whispering? Explain your thoughts clearly."

Narada replied, "This is a very delicate instrument.
It is very dear to me. It is as dear to me as life itself. He
is a monkey. He will spoil my instrument entirely."

Lord Krishna said, "Do not be afraid, beloved Rishi!
Give it to him. I will be held responsible for your
veena."

Narada gave the *veena* to the monkey-chief reluctantly. Sri Hanuman was not a bit affected by the
insulting words of the Rishi. He was a sage of balanced
mind and great self-control.

Thereupon the Lord said, "O monkey-chief! let us
hear your charming music."

Hanuman started singing Ram-Nam with intense
devotion and began playing on the *veena*. It excelled
Narada's music. The listeners were immensely
pleased with it. The music of Hanuman even melted
the stones. All praised him. Narada also joined them.

Lord Krishna said, "O Rishi! it is good that you also
appreciated the music of the monkey-chief. It was
indeed astounding."

Narada hung his head in shame and at once fell at
the feet of the Lord, saying, "O Lord! please forgive me.
How can I judge the merits of men? Thou art
omniscient. Thou art the real judge."

Narada tried to take back his *veena* but discovered
that he could not raise it from the ground. He said to
the Lord, "O Lord! I cannot lift my *veena* from the

ground. The monkey has played a trick on me. Let me have the *veena* back."

Lord Krishna said, "O Narada! let others try to lift it up."

Everyone tried, but in vain. The Lord then enquired from the other musicians as to the cause of the sticking of the *veena*. A highly skilful musician remarked, "The stone on which the *veena* was placed melted through the music of the monkey-chief and thus it sank a little; when the music stopped it hardened again and the *veena* got stuck."

Lord Krishna said, "O Rishi Narada! sing and melt the stone and take back your *veena*."

Narada sang and sang to his level best, but his efforts proved futile. Then Lord Krishna asked Hanuman to continue singing and playing the *veena*. The stone melted within a few minutes. Narada took back his *veena*.

Narada discovered that Lord Krishna had devised this plan to remove his pride. He came to know that the monkey-chief was none other than Sri Hanuman. He embraced Sri Hanuman with great affection, at the same time apologising for his misbehaviour.

Narada's music pride was thus quelled and he returned a better man. At times the Lord makes fun of His devotees.

Pride is the greatest drawback in man. It is a dire evil and very diifficult to eradicate. Even the best of men fall prey to it. It mars one's achievements. Just as a beautiful painting is entirely spoilt by an ugly black mark on it, so also pride completely spoils one's life, however great be one's talents, accomplishments and achievements. Give up pride through humility and Sadhana.

15

THE REWARD OF FAITH

A LITTLE PRINCE, richly bedecked with jewels, was standing near a pond. The old, bearded robber came along, reflecting the evil intent that filled his heart. He pretended to collapse on the ground and uttered a piteous cry. The prince, true to his kingly nature, rushed to the old man and enquired of his health.

"I am dying of thirst, child. Please get some water to drink."

"I shall do so at once," replied the prince and went towards the pond.

"Not thus, sweet child; the water you give might be the last sip I have in this life. You have not had initiation and so you have not experienced the Presence of God. If only you could be initiated into the holy word, which will compel God Himself to appear before you, the water you give will become sanctified, fit to be drunk by me, a holy man, at the time of departing from this world."

"Kindly initiate me into the Mantra, sir," said the boy.

"Go and immerse yourself in that pond, son," said the old man. "But before you go, take off those costly jewels and apparel and leave them on the shore. Hold your breath and keep your head under water till I call out to you. In the meantime I shall go on repeating the purificatory Mantras to make the initiation highly efficacious."

The innocent boy did as he was told. The ornaments were at the old man's feet, filling his heart with great joy. The boy got into the water and as he immersed his head, the robber took all the jewels and fled.

The boy was made of sterner stuff. Precious minutes passed, but the Guru's call did not come. He did not want to raise his head from the water before the Guru called out. Conscious struggle almost led to unconsciousness. Instead of vital breath he inhaled cold water.

The young devotee's steadfastness and utter self-surrender moved the heart of Lord Narayana. He left His divine abode and rushed to where the prince was.

Standing near the pond, the Lord called out to the prince, "My child, I am Lord Narayana, the Lord of the universe. I am highly pleased with your devotion. Kindly come out of the water now."

But the boy wouldn't! Mentally he said to himself, "Whoever you might be, I cannot raise my head from the water till my Guru calls out to me."

Lord Narayana hurried to where the robber was. Disguising Himself as a police officer and father of the boy, the Lord caught hold of the robber, belaboured him and said, "You have compelled my boy to remain under water till you call, and he won't get out till you do so. Go! Run and call him out at once."

They both went to the pond. The robber called out to the boy, "Oh child, come! Come out of the water now."

The Reward of Faith

As the boy raised his head, the robber dropped dead. The boy had the supreme reward for his intense faith and devotion and spirit of self-surrender. He had the vision of Lord Narayana.

16

HOW A SAGE RULED

IN A CERTAIN COUNTRY there was a practice in days
of yore that when the king died without leaving an
heir, the ministers would let loose a special palace
elephant. It would catch hold of anyone it liked and
place him on its head. That man would then be
crowned king without any further question.

Once it happened that the elephant caught hold of a
Sannyasin, a realised sage of true renunciation. He
was brought to the court with all pomp and ceremony.

The Sannyasin was puzzled and asked the
ministers, "What is the matter? Why have you brought
me here?"

"Sir, you are to be crowned king. This is the custom
here. You have been chosen by the palace elephant."

"No, no, I do not want any kind of kingdom. I am a
Sannyasin."

"Please do not disappoint us," pleaded the
ministers. They pursuaded him to ascend the throne.
The saint reluctantly agreed.

The saint-monarch was indifferent to whatever
went on in the kingdom. In spite of it everything went
on smoothly and prosperity reigned.

How a Sage Ruled

A neighbouring ruler, hearing of the nature of the new king, thought it a good opportunity to invade his kingdom and capture it.

The ministers informed the saint-monarch of his intention.

"Why does he wish to invade our kingdom? What have we done to him?"

"We do not know. There is no apparent cause. His armies are marching into our territory. Please order us. We will go and fight them."

"No, no. Keep quiet. Why should we fight?"

The ministers were puzzled. They did not know what to do. Finding that the saint-king's forces had not come for battle, the enemy ruler himself came to the saint-king's Durbar. The saint-king was quite indifferent.

The enemy king spoke to him, "O Rajah! I have come here to fight you. What do you have to say now?"

"What do you gain by that? Why do you want to fight with us?"

"I want to capture your kingdom."

"O ruler! you need not fight with my armies for that. You can take this throne. I am only a Sannyasin. I was always a Sannyasin. I will go away. Come on, ascend this throne. From now on you are the ruler of this kingdom also."

So saying, the Sannyasin, in a peaceful mood started walking away.

The enemy king was abashed. In utter bewilderment he prostrated before the saint-king, begged his pardon and offered his own kingdom instead of taking the saint's. The saint became the ruler of both the kingdoms!

The ministers who were sitting with awe-stricken

65

faces were illumined. They understood the power of renunciation. A whole nation was saved from bloodshed, and the saint won a kingdom without asking for it!

17

YOU CAN'T DECEIVE GOD

RAMAKRISHNAN WAS studying for his matriculation. His English was weak. So he neglected mathematics and paid more attention to this subject. The day before the English exam he had to write mathematics. As he was not quite prepared, he was a bit worried. Failure seemed to be almost certain.

There was a temple near the school. He had faith that God could do anything, even the impossible. Before the mathematics paper was to be answered, he went to the temple and prayed: "O Lord! help me to pass in this subject. If I am able to answer the papers satisfactorily I will offer you *prasad* worth Rs. 20."

And the miracle happened. All the questions on the paper were easy for him. They were all worked out with ease and perfection. Not only success, but brilliant success was his. He had answered all the questions correctly and he knew it. Besides this, he had not taken even half the allotted time to complete the paper. He was overjoyed.

Ramakrishnan had time to spare. To utilise it he thought he would prepare a list of the articles that would be necessary for the *prasad*. The estimate was

Rs. 20. After completing the list he reflected: "One or two items are not really essential. Why waste money after all?" He cut them out and the estimate came down to Rs. 15. Then, revising the estimate again, he said to himself: "Is God a businessman, granting success in exams in return for Rs. 15 worth of *prasad*? I need not be worried over the actual amount. After offering the *prasad* to Him, my friends and I only are going to take it. So why spend so much on it."

The estimate came down to Rs. 5, and on further revision, to Rs. 2. A verse from the *Gita* now came to his mind. He thought: "Has not the Lord declared in the *Gita* that He accepts with delight a leaf, a flower, a fruit or even mere water offered to Him with faith and devotion? After all, it is the devotion and the feeling of the heart that matters. I can get the same merit of offering Rs. 20 worth of *prasad* as by offering with devotion two good plantain fruits."

As he was reflecting thus, the bell rang and the hall supervisor came to him for his answer papers. With a broad and happy smile on his face, Ramakrishnan gave the papers to the supervisor and went home, confident that he had achieved amazing success in the subject.

"But what is this? You have brought the answer papers home!" exclaimed his father, looking at the bunch of papers in the boy's hand.

To his horror, Ramakrishnan realised that in his absent-minded hurry when the bell rang, he had gathered the "*prasad* estimate" papers together and given them to the supervisor, and by mistake had brought the real answer papers home! He would get nothing but a good "0"!

Ramakrishnan wept bitterly. "O father! by the

68

You Can't Deceive God

Grace of God I had done wonderfully well in the subject, but my wicked mind had begun to think of cheating God by escaping from the *prasad* expenses. Even philosophical arguments seemed to support my unfaithful action. This is the result."

His father said, "You cannot deceive God."

18

DARIDRANARAYANA'S PRAYER

THERE HAS NOT BEEN on earth a man poorer than Daridranarayana. He had a large family with no property, no earnings, except the meagre yield of two cows. The cows themselves would not yield even an ounce of milk unless they got a pound of husk.

One day Daridranarayana's son tripped and fell into a well while he was bringing the pot of husk. Both son and husk were gone. Daridranarayana was disgusted. He ran away from the house, bound for Rishikesh.

On the way he met a great Yogi meditating underneath a tree. He bowed to the Yogi. The Yogi opened his eyes and saw Daridranarayana, who related his tale of woe and asked for the Yogi's blessings. The Yogi gave him initiation into the Kubera Mantra.

Daridranarayana did Japa of the Mantra. Kubera appeared before him and said, "Ask whatever you want."

Daridranarayana quickly replied, "Give me four seers of husk."

Kubera laughed at his stupidity, gave him the husk and disappeared. When he heard of it, the Yogi said, "What a great fool you are! When the God of Wealth

70

Daridranarayana's Prayer

appeared before you, you asked only for four seers of husk. Truly, you are like the Bhakta who prays to the Lord of the three worlds for petty wealth or worldly prosperity instead of eternal bliss and everlasting peace."

19

SVARNAKESA

ONCE UPON a time there lived a Mahatma in a beautiful valley of the Himalayas. He had a small cottage made of grass on the banks of the river Bhagirathi. He was content with what he got by chance and was leading a very happy life, spending his time in divine contemplation.

It so happened that one fine morning the thought entered his mind that he should leave his Himalayan solitude and enter the plains and lead a mendicant's life, wandering from place to place.

So he entered the plains. People were struck by his magnetic spiritual aura. He impressed them by his actions, speech and advice. His charming personality attracted all. He had grown a beautiful beard and had flowing hair, the colour of gold. On account of this he came to be known as Svarnakesa.

As Swami Svarnakesa wended his way through the plains he impressed one and all by his personality. One day he was passing through a village. A lady approached him in tears with a child in her arms. She narrated her awful tale of how six of her children had died one after another. She appealed to the Mahatma to save her seventh child who was seriously suffering from high fever.

Svarnakesa

Swami Svarnakesa felt pity for the woman and consoled her. He then pulled out one of the hairs from his head and said, "O venerable lady! take this hair. Preserve it carefully and your child will be all right."

The lady took leave of the Mahatma in great joy. By God's Grace the child soon recovered. The news spread everywhere. The Mahatma became very popular. The citizens of the towns and villages all around came to know that there was a Mahatma who could cure the diseases of children by his magical hair. The news spread like wild fire.

The number of devotees who visited him grew more and more. Thousands of women approached him with their children for blessings. For all deserving cases the Mahatma would pull out a hair from his head and bless the patient with a sure cure.

As days passed, the number of patients increased. There was a regular cry for the Mahatma's hair. Svarnakesa could not cope with the crowd. They could not wait for the Mahatma to pull out his hair from his head.

At last the excited crowd got hold of him and forcibly pulled out all his hair one by one. The Mahatma yelled in agony. People in their anxiety to get themselves cured of their diseases did not mind his anguish, until at last, the poor Svarnakesa breathed his last with wounds all over his body.

A spiritual aspirant should not run after name and fame. He should not run after powers. Flying in the air, drinking nitric acid, swallowing nails, walking on fire, entering into Samadhi on public platforms, burying oneself alive for forty days—these are not the true tests of a Jivanmukta or Siddha.

A Yogi is not one who shows some miraculous

73

feats. A Siddha or Mahatma is not to be tested merely by the wearing of a loin-cloth, or by living in icy regions, or by eating *neem* leaves, or by living on air and water only. The real test of a Mahatma lies in the peace that he radiates, the joy and bliss that he imparts to those around him. The good that he does for humanity, the peace and bliss that he himself enjoys, absence of anger, lust, greed and desire for name and fame, equanimity in success and failure, cheerfulness, unalloyed bliss, absence of cares, worries and anxieties—know a true Mahatma by such sterling qualities.

A Mahatma is a Kalpa Vriksha. He bestows everything on his devotees. The extent of his power depends upon the degree of devotion he possesses. A Mahatma is a Chintamani. One can get anything and everything from him. Qualify yourself. Purify yourself. Empty yourself. He will then fill you with realisation, light, joy, prosperity, immortality and bliss.

May the blessings of Mahatmas be ever upon you! May you become blessed to receive their Grace!

20

THE TEST OF RENUNCIATION

TWO SADHUS dwelt in a holy place. One was a multi-millionaire before he renounced. Even after he became a Sadhu, his children had volunteered to look after his physical needs and therefore he had servants and all comforts and conveniences. The other Sadhu was leading an extremely austere life. He lived on alms and had absolutely no possessions except the clothes he wore, a water-pot and a deer skin. He lead a very austere life.

The poor Sadhu used to admire himself for his spirit of renunciation and laugh at the rich Sadhu. He would even speak disparagingly of the latter whenever he met other Mahatmas or devotees.

"He must have found himself too old to carry on the life of a householder, so he has made a pretence of renouncing the world and embracing Sannyasa. See the luxury he revels in!"

This spark of pride and contempt grew in time into a big conflagration and the poor Sadhu proudly approached the rich Sadhu one day and, sermonising on renunciation, said, "What a great power there is in renunciation! But it must be real and genuine, like mine. You have no doubt renounced wealth and family. But when are you going to renounce this luxurious living?"

"Just now, Narayan. Come, let us go to Uttarkasi!" replied the rich Sadhu instantly.

The poor Sadhu was taken by surprise. His pride and eagerness to prove that the rich Sadhu's offer was a sham, made him follow him. They went a mile or two and as they were leaving the outskirts of the village, the poor Sadhu suddenly remembered that he had left his water-pot and deer skin behind. He said, "Sir, please wait. I have to go and fetch my water-pot and deer skin."

The rich Sadhu gave a significant smile.

What is real renunciation? It is renunciation of attachment, delusion, "I"-ness and "mine"-ness. The luxurious Sadhu was ready to give up everything in a moment; the poor Sadhu clung to his water-pot and deer skin.

21

TRUE KARMA YOGA

ONCE A SHOE AND a lump of *halwa* (a kind of confectionery) approached a sage and placed before him their grievances.

The shoe said, "O adorable sage! listen to my pitiable lot. I carry my master day and night over dirty, stony and thorny surfaces. On account of his weight I constantly wear out. But my master does not have the courtesy to take me into his house. He leaves me outside the door always. I am not able to bear this insult. My master does not appreciate my service even a bit."

The sage replied, "O beloved shoe! you are indeed a great Karma Yogi. You serve your master at great personal sacrifice. You protect the master's feet from thorns and stones by covering his foot in yourself and enduring all hardships. You are certainly an embodiment of sacrifice. All glory to you! But you do not seem to have correctly understood the technique of Karma Yoga. A Karma Yogi should perform his work in a spirit of divine worship, without the least expectation of any personal gain, not even appreciation for the work he does. A Karma Yogi should feel that he is serving the Lord in the person whom he is attending upon. Far from expecting appreciation from the person served, the Karma Yogi should be thankful to the person for having given him an opportunity of serving the Lord in him.

"Do not feel that you are serving your master's feet but feel that you are serving God in the master. God is in all forms. All are manifestations of God only. Further, shun honour and respect. A Karma Yogi should treat honour and dishonour alike. He should maintain balance of mind under all circumstances. If you continue treating all work as the worship of God Himself, expecting no fruits, nor even recognition, and treating honour and dishonour, pain and pleasure, gain and loss alike, you will doubtlessly earn God's supreme Grace and enjoy eternal bliss. Therefore, go back and continue your work."

The lump of *halwa* then laid its complaint before the sage. It said, "O revered sage! kindly listen to my pathetic tale. I look appealing and sweet-smelling in the sweetmeat shop. No passer-by goes away without casting a fond glance at me. People like me so much that my aroma or the very mention of my name makes their mouths water. No important feast or festival takes place without my presence. But alas! a strange transformation takes place in me after I have been eaten by people. Several hours after I am eaten, I am discarded in a changed form very dirty and foul-smelling. People shun me. They spit on the ground or close their nostrils when they see me. I am unable to bear this insult."

The sage replied, "O beloved sweetmeat! you too are a great Karma Yogi like the shoe. With your nutritive elements, you serve those who eat you. You sacrifice your beauty, sweet aroma, honour and your very form itself in order to nourish and sustain people and satisfy their palate. What an embodiment of selfless service you are! But do not weep over the change that comes to your physical form, for you are not this physical form. You are neither the beautiful, attractive *halwa* nor the foul-smelling excreta. You are an embodiment of the spirit of selfless service. This spirit lives through the ages and is sought as an ideal by great souls. It is unaffected by the changes and the impurities of the physical form. Identify yourself not with the material form, but stand as a witness of its functions and continue to serve people with your nutritious and taste-giving elements. Service done without the idea of agency but as a witness is the ideal of a Karma Yogi. It is an immortal ideal that makes you very happy. Identification with the physical form is the root cause of suffering and sorrow."

Thus comforted, both the shoe and the lump of *halwa* returned to their respective abodes, serving the people as instructed by the sage and did not complain thereafter.

22

GOD-REALISATION THROUGH YUKTI

RAM LAL HAD led a life of sin. Countless were the sins committed by him. In fact, during his whole lifetime he had performed only one act of charity, one virtuous act, and that was to feed a hungry Mahatma, a God-realised saint.

When he was dying, a messenger of Lord Yama, the God of Death, came to take him away and asked, "Ram Lal, you have a mountain of sins whose evil fruits you have to eat, and you have one virtuous act whose joyous fruit also you can enjoy. Now choose which you would prefer first—the enjoyment of the result of the one virtuous act or the suffering of the results of your numerous sins."

"O Deva! let me finish off the enjoyment of the fruit of the virtuous act first. Then I will go on suffering in hell for the sins I have committed."

The messenger took Ram Lal to heaven. Ram Lal could get there whatever he wanted. He was told that his one virtuous act was so great that he could go anywhere in the three worlds—he could enter the gates of Vaikuntha or Kailasa and have the Darshan of the Lord, or he could enjoy all the pleasures of heaven.

God-realisation Through Yukti

Ram Lal was very intelligent. He saw his opportunity in this.

He got on to the Divine Horse, Devendra, and went about the three worlds. Finally, when his term in heaven was about to come to an end, he went to Vaikuntha and had the Darshan of the Lord Himself.

As he was coming out of Vaikuntha the messengers of hell approached him with the words, "Ram Lal, your merits are now exhausted. Come to hell and suffer for the bad Karmas."

"What!" replied Ram Lal, "can a man who has had Darshan of the Lord be taken to hell? O Narayana!"

Immediately the messengers of Lord Narayana appeared and drove away the messengers of hell. Ram Lal remained forever at the Lord's Feet!

23

THE WISDOM OF THE MONGOOSE

VIVEKAMATI WAS a very virtuous youth living in the country of Kalinga. He was living with his Guru, serving him and studying and acquiring knowledge of the *Vedas*.

Having completed his period of studentship, Vivekamati was preparing to leave his Gurukula abode. He approached his preceptor and addressed him thus: "O venerable Master! living with thee in this pure and sacred abode, I was safe from the temptations and dangerous attractions of the world. I have now to leave this sheltered place and go amidst the strife and battle of secular life. Pray, tell me how I may save myself from the terrible onslaught of worldliness and Maya. Show me a method."

The wise Guru reflected for a while and said, "Come, I shall show thee the proper means of safeguarding thyself. Follow me now."

So saying, the Guru led the way, followed by the eager Vivekamati. They reached a small clearing in the midst of a thick jungle. Here lived a bold and powerful mongoose named Sukavachee or the "well-armoured". He was very agile and constantly alert, because the forest was infested with all kinds of fierce serpents with deadly venom. Daily the mongoose had to fight its foes.

When the Guru and Vivekamati entered the glade, such a fight was in progress. The mongoose was facing the serpent and never took its eyes off its foe. Every time it was attacked, the serpent tried to grip the mongoose in its powerful coils. The mongoose never got caught due to its agility. But at times it was bitten by the snake. The fight went on and at intervals the mongoose vanished into the surrounding thicket and again emerged fresh and vigorous as ever, quite free from all trace of wound or injury. It was never finally exhausted though the snake was seen to weaken and gradually lose its ferocity. The mongoose killed the snake in the end and emerged triumphant and unscathed.

Vivekamati, watching all this in silent wonderment, at last turned to his Guru for enlightenment. The Guru said, "Did you observe, O Vivekamati! the fight between the mongoose and the serpent? Such is the struggle of man with the deadly serpent of worldliness. Even as the mongoose did, man must keep a constant and alert watchfulness lest the coils of worldliness take him unawares.

"Keep the twin eyes of discrimination and enquiry wide open. At times you may become poisoned in the course of your life in the world. Then, just as the mongoose disappeared into the jungle and revived itself with the *sanjivini* herb and came back again to the fray, you too must retire periodically from the worldly atmosphere and take recourse to Satsang, Sadhana, seclusion and silent meditation. Satsang and seclusion are the magic herbs which remove the poison of worldliness from you. With their help you can keep yourself safe, O Vivekamati! Depart now with courage. Have no fear."

Hearing this, Vivekamati was quite reassured and prostrated before the Guru and took his leave. He lived the life of an ideal householder, without at all falling a prey to worldliness. After a noble, unattached life in the world he took to Sannyasa, did intense austerities and attained salvation.

Periodical seclusion, Sadhana and Satsang are thus life-giving herbs to aspirants struggling in the world. May they be saved by never neglecting these!

24

THOTAKACHARYA

SRI SANKARACHARYA, the exponent of the Kevala Adwaita philosophy had four great disciples. They were Padmapada, Hasthamalaka, Sureswaracharya and Thotakacharya.

Thotaka was a dull type of student but he was intensely devoted to Sri Sankara. He rendered all kinds of services to his Guru.

One day the *Brahma Sutra* class was about to be started. The devoted disciple took a little extra time to cleanse the clothes of his Guru in the river. The other disciples pressed Sri Sankaracharya to commence the class without Thotakacharya.

They said to him, "Thotakacharya is a dull student. He cannot understand the *Brahma Sutras*. Let us start the class. There is no use in waiting for him as he cannot understand the profound and subtle significance of the verses."

Sri Sankaracharya wanted to teach a lesson to these proud disciples. He at once showered his Grace on the devoted Thotakacharya. Thotakacharya had immediate illumination. Knowledge dawned in him. He came to the class exclaiming: "O ocean of the nectar of illumined knowledge of the whole *Shastras*! Thou hast revealed to me the treasure of the meaning of the great *Upanishads*. I meditate on thy pure lotus feet in my heart. O Sankara, my teacher! be thou my refuge. I meditate on thee, who expounded the identity of the Jiva and Ishwara. O Sankara! thou art my God! I am therefore full of joy. Thou hast dried up the ocean filled with the waters of infatuation in me. O Sankara, my spiritual guide! It is by the result of great virtuous deeds performed by me for a long time that I have in me a love for the vision of thy lotus feet. Protect this humble self, O Sankara, my spiritual preceptor!"

Padmapada and the other disciples were struck with amazement. Their pride was quelled at once.

Service of the Guru is a supreme blessing. Devotion to the Guru is a great purifier of the heart. Guru's Grace alone can help the aspirant to cross this formidable ocean of worldliness. The Guru is Brahma, Guru is Vishnu, Guru is Siva, Guru is Brahman.

Glory to the Guru! May the blessings of Brahma Vidya Gurus be upon you all!

25

DURBUDDHI

DURBUDDHI WAS an atheist in the city of Gaya. He lived during the time of Lord Buddha.

Durbuddhi was a very cruel man. He tormented good people. He robbed them, terrorised them and caused fear. He was a fierce personality. Children and women were struck with terror at the mere mention of his name. He was a demon in human form.

One day, Durbuddhi approached Lord Buddha when he was seated in meditation. When Buddha opened his eyes, he saw Durbuddhi standing in front of him.

The saint greeted him; Durbuddhi abused Buddha in return. He used the most objectionable language in abusing Lord Buddha.

He said to him, "O fool! you are an imposter. You are a cheat. You are a hypocrite. You are a rogue in the guise of a saint. Get away from this place. If you come here tomorrow, I shall kill you. The city is full of beggars and imposters like you. They have spoilt the whole country. You are a mere idler. You are a burden on society. You drain the resources of householders who earn their livelihood with the sweat of their brow through hard labour."

Buddha heard all this and kept silent. The next day also Durbuddhi came and abused Buddha in similar vulgar words with added fury. Even then Lord Buddha kept quiet. This process repeated itself for over a month. As days passed on, Durbuddhi became more and more furious.

At last he said one day, "O man! are you deaf? Do you not hear what I say? You sit like a block of stone in spite of my abuses. You are a shameless creature. Tell me what sort of man you are."

Buddha coolly replied, "I have been all along hearing what you spoke. I am not deaf. But I may tell you that I have not accepted any of your insults. When I have not accepted them, to whom do they belong? You gave me some presents, but I decline to accept them."

Saying this Buddha kept silent.

Durbuddhi's mind was at once changed by the calmness of the sage. He was thoroughly transformed. He fell at Buddha's feet and cried, "O Lord! pardon me. I am a vile wretch. I have wronged you, a pure and godly personality. What a great crime I have committed! Again and again I entreat you to pardon me. Thou art an ocean of mercy! Forgive me!"

Durbuddhi then became a follower of the great Buddha.

Friends, learn patience from Buddha. Be noble and magnanimous. Rise above censure and praise. You are very weak. You cannot bear the insult of your own brother. If anyone speaks a little harsh word you are upset at once. You are wild with fury. What are censure and praise? They are mere vibrations in the ether. Do not attach any importance to them. Be even-minded in pleasure and pain, in success and defeat, censure and praise, heat and cold. Bear insult and injury. You will become an Emperor of emperors, a Shah of shahs.

May God bless you with inner spiritual strength to conquer anger and impatience!

26

THE UNGRATEFUL DOG

IN A CERTAIN LARGE forest there lived an ascetic who
practised rigid vows. He lived on fruits and roots. He
had control of his senses. He purified his heart
through fasts. He treated all creatures with intense
affection. When he sat on his seat all the animals used
to approach him with affection on account of his
mercy and goodness of conduct.

Ferocious lions, tigers, leopards and elephants used
to come to the Rishi. All of them behaved towards him
like disciples and slaves and always did what was
agreeable to him.

A dog resided with the saint permanently. It was
greatly attached to the ascetic. It lived on fruits and
roots also. It became weak and emaciated on account
of fasts.

Ond day a very strong and hungry leopard came
there to eat the dog. The dog ran to the Rishi for
protection. The Rishi took pity on the dog and at once
transformed it into a leopard more powerful than the
newcomer. The leopard went away in great disappointment.

Sometime later a dreadful tiger came to attack the
dog that was now changed into a leopard. The leopard

sought the Rishi's protection once again. This time the Rishi transformed the leopard into a powerful tiger. The other tiger, like the first leopard, also went away in disappointment.

The dog that was transformed into a tiger left off its former food of fruits and roots and began to live on other animals of the forest like a true king of beasts.

A huge elephant now came to attack the tiger. The tiger once again sought shelter at the feet of the Rishi. Thereupon the Rishi transformed the tiger into an elephant more powerful than the real elephant. The real elephant departed in fear.

One day a lion came to attack the elephant. Once again the Rishi changed the elephant, which was formerly a dog, into a lion stronger than his new enemy. Seeing a stronger beast of his own species, the wild lion became afraid and ran away.

Sometime later a Sharabha (a fierce wild animal) with eight legs and eyes on the forehead, came to kill the dog that had been transformed into a lion. The Rishi took pity on the dog-lion and turned it into a very strong Sharabha. Seeing the Rishi's Sharabha before him more powerful than himself, the wild Sharabha at once fled in fear out of the forest.

Now the Sharabha became free of all danger. He lived happily, but all the other animals lived in terror.

One day, the ungrateful beast, which had once been a dog and was now transformed into a Sharabha by the saint, eagerly thirsted for the blood of the Rishi. The Rishi understood this through his spiritual vision and ascetic power.

The saint said, "O dog! I transformed you into various forms in order to save you from danger. I had great love for you. O sinful wretch! you now wish to kill

91

me who have done no injury to you. You will assume the form of your own species and be a dog again."

The mean, wicked and foolish animal once again put on his own proper form of a dog.

People who are endowed with gratitude are rare in this world. It is not proper to forget the good done to you by others. You should be ever grateful to that man who has done you good and who has served you when you were in difficulty.

27

THE POWER OF CHASTITY

THERE WAS ONCE a high-class Brahmana, known by the name of Kaushika, who was a student of the *Vedas*. He was rich with the wealth of devotion. He was endowed with virtuous behaviour.

One day, Kaushika sat at the foot of a tree and recited the *Vedas*. A crane, sitting on the tree above, passed some excrement on the body of the Brahmana. The Brahmana was very much enraged. He looked at the crane. It fell down on the ground lifeless, destroyed by the power of his anger.

Presently, Kaushika entered a village for alms. He approached a house and asked for alms. The lady of the house said, "Kindly wait, I shall attend on you soon."

While she was cleaning the vessel to give the alms, her husband suddenly entered the house, oppressed by great hunger.

The chaste lady served her husband with food and drink and stood by to attend to all his needs. She had to make Kaushika wait unnecessarily.

The lady was highly devoted to her husband. She daily ate the remnants of her husband's dish. She regarded him as her lord. She was always engaged in serving her lord. She was virtuous. She had good behaviour. She was beneficient to her relatives.

The highly devoted lady was always attentive to what was beneficial to her husband. She daily attended to the service of the guests, the mother-in-law, the father-in-law and the servants. She was pure and chaste.

After serving her husband the chaste lady came with alms for the Brahmana. Kaushika was much enraged.

The lady said, "O learned one! forgive me. My husband is my chief god. He was very hungry and fatigued. Finding him thus, I served him first."

The Brahmana said, "The Brahmanas are not regarded by you as superior. You regard your husband to be superior to all. Living a domestic life, you disrespect the Brahmanas. Even Indra bows down to them. Do you know or have you not heard from elders that the Brahmanas are really like fire and can burn the whole earth?"

The woman said, "O Brahmana! O thou who art possessed of the wealth of asceticism! Do not consider that I am a crane. What will you do to me by your angry look? Really I never disrespect the Brahmanas, who are like celestials themselves. You should forgive my fault. I know the power of Brahmanas.

"By their wrath the ocean is made brackish and undrinkable. The evil-minded Vatapi, a crooked Asura, was digested by sage Agastya. The sages possess immense wrath, but they also possess a good deal of forgiveness. It behoves you to forgive me in this matter of my transgression. The merit that is derived from the worship of my husband is liked by me. Of all the gods, my husband is my highest Deity. I cultivate that special virtue—the service of my husband—as the

94

highest good. I know that the female crane was burnt by your anger, but such wrath is one's mortal enemy. The gods know him to be a Brahmana who abandons his wrath, who speaks the truth, and who comforts the preceptor. The gods know him to be a Brahmana, who, being himself injured, never injures others, and who keeps his passions under his perfect control, who is holy, virtuous and ever devoted to the study of the *Vedas*.

"The gods know him to be a Brahmana who has control over wrath and desires, and who again, acquainted with virtue and possessed of energy, considers every man to be equal to him.

"The gods know him to be a Brahmana who is conversant with all systems of religion, who studies himself and teaches, and who again performs sacrifices himself and presides at the sacrifices performed by others.

"The gods know him to be a Brahmana who gives away according to his means, who is liberal and who always attends to his studies.

"Those persons who are versed in morality consider the subduing of the senses, truth and simplicity of behaviour to be the eternal and highest virtues.

"Virtue is eternal and difficult of attainment. It is established upon truth. Virtue, again, rests entirely upon the *Srutis*, which are the utterances of venerable sages.

'Virtue seems to be varied and true. You do not know the real essence of virtue, O Brahmana! O regenerate one! if you do not know the highest virtue, go to the city of Mithila, and there ask the virtuous fowler, who ever serves his father and mother, who is truthful, and who has control over passions. He will explain to you

95

the different systems of religion. If you like, O blessed one! you may go there.

"Remember, O Brahmana! that the woman who is greatly devoted to the practice of virtues is incapable of being injured."

The Brahmana said, "O beauteous lady! be happy. I am much pleased with you. My wrath has now subsided. The chiding uttered by you will prove most beneficial to me. I shall go to Mithila and perform what is advantageous to me."

Then Kaushika, the foremost of the twice-born ones, came out and, chiding himself, returned to his house.

28

AN OBEDIENT WIFE

TEK CHAND, a devotee of Kabir, was talking with the Master one afternoon. Kabir was explaining to him the various methods one should adopt for realising God by leading the life of a householder.

Kabir went on to explain: "You can convert your own home into heaven if only you wish to do so and act in the manner prescribed in the *Shastras*."

Tek Chand was surprised. "What, Maharaj! Home into heaven? I have heard it said that it is impossible and that man can realise God only by resorting to forests and doing austerities for many years. They say that wife, children and possessions are all formidable obstacles on the way of an aspirant's progress towards his goal. It greatly surprises me to hear this statement from you—that our own home can be converted into heaven."

"Yes, I shall explain it to you," said Kabir. "It is very simple. An obedient wife is all that is needed to accomplish this task. If she treats her husband as God Himself and acts according to his wishes, without even a second thought, she has the power of converting the home into heaven. By doing so she not only realises the goal of life herself, but enables her husband also to attain God-realisation. The children too become beaconlights of wisdom and great Yogis.

"I see doubt expressed on your face. If you are not convinced come to my house one of these days and I will make you understand the truth behind what I say."

After about a week, Tek Chand paid a surprise visit to Kabir's house. Kabir was weaving cloth. His wife was busy with the work on the thread. Kabir rose from his seat, welcomed Tek Chand with *pranam* and made him sit at his side. After enquiring about Tek Chand's health, the welfare of his family and the progress of his Sadhana, Kabir asked his wife to bring some clay.

Without a word, she left the room and brought the clay. Next he asked her to bring some *ghee*; this too was brought at once. Kabir then requested his wife to pour the *ghee* into the clay and mix both well. Without even a sign of astonishment at the mysterious behaviour of her husband, she did as she was told to do. She was then asked to make small balls of this clay mixture and cook them in the frying-pan.

Tek Chand looked on all this dumbfounded. When the fried balls were ready, Kabir asked his wife to throw them away. This was done also.

Tek Chand could not understand what all this meant. He thought that perhaps it was the custom in Kabir's family. Kabir and his wife resumed their work.

Tek Chand enquired, "Maharaj, you promised the other day that you would show me an easy method of converting home into heaven. Would it suit you to fulfil that promise today?"

Kabir replied, "Why, you have already seen a most practical demonstration of what I said. It was for your sake that I wasted so much *ghee*, time and labour. You have not understood yet the meaning of the demonstration.

Tek Chand replied, "Is that all? My wife also can do likewise. Is this all that is required to convert a home into heaven?"

"Yes, try it then," advised Kabir. "You will experience the result yourself."

Tek Chand returned home and immediately wished to try the experiment. His wife was in her room playing cards with some of her friends. Tek Chand was impatient; he shouted for her half a dozen times before even getting a reply. When she came, murmuring at the intrusion of her husband, he told her that he had something very urgent to be done by her and asked her to dissolve the party.

She refused, but on persuasion, agreed to finish the play "in a few minutes".

Tek Chand sat in his room counting time and planning his adventure.

When, after taking leave of her friends, his wife reappeared before him, Tek Chand asked her to get some clay.

Indira: "Good heavens! What are you going to do with clay at this time of the day? And is this the urgent business for which you spoilt my play?"

Tek Chand: "Don't argue with me now. Please bring some clay."

The clay is brought.

Indira: "Here is the clay. Now I am going back to my friends. Meanwhile you verify if this is the same substance as is in your head just now."

She turns towards the door.

Tek Chand: "Don't go away. My business is not over. Bring me some *ghee*."

Indira: "You look curious today. Your talk is equally curious. Are you in your senses? Or if you are feeling a bit out of sorts, shall I send for the doctor?"

Take Chand: "Nothing is the matter with me. You will yourself know a few minutes later why I am asking you to do all this. Please bring me a little *ghee*."

Indira: "All right, please yourself."

Brings a little *ghee*.

Indira: "What are you going to do with this?"

Tek Chand: "Going to convert this home into a heaven."

Indira: "Ha! Ha! Turn this home into heaven! It already is—if only I get my companions back. You are mad. I thought as much at the very first sight when you arrived home today."

Tek Chand: "Don't be silly. Pour the *ghee* into that clay."

Indira (growing wild): "What! I am not going to waste the precious *ghee* to satisfy the fancy of a madman like you. I am still in my proper senses. Do you think that I have also gone mad? Are you drunk or what? Go into your room and lie down for a couple of hours. Then you will be all right."

Takes the ghee and goes to the door.

Tek Chand (preventing her from going out): "Do as I tell you. Don't ask questions. Don't argue. Otherwise I shall beat you."

Indira: "What do you mean? I am not going to waste the *ghee* and pour it on the mud."

Tek Chand (vehemently): "If you do not do as I order you, I shall beat you severely. Don't you want our house to become a heaven?"

Indira: "Who put these queer ideas into your head? If you want you can go to the bazaar and get some *ghee* and pour it wherever you like. I won't allow you to waste this *ghee* which I have specially prepared myself. Going to convert the home into heaven!"

Tek Chand beats her.

Indira: "O Kamala, Vasantha, Sulochana! my husband has gone mad. He is beating me. Please come to my rescue. He will kill me now."

The neighbours rush into the house. Kabir also walks in. They catch hold of Tek Chand and make him sit on a bench.

Nandlal (a neighbour): "What is the matter, Tek Chand? Why are you . . ."

Indira: "Oh! he has gone mad today. Please ask someone to remove him to the mental hospital or he will murder me."

Tek Chand: "No, I am not mad, Nandlal. I wanted to convert this home into heaven. She would not co-operate with me."

Nandlal: "What! How do you propose to convert the home into heaven?"

Tek Chand: "You see, if a wife dutifully and implicitly obeys her husband, the home in which they live will be turned into heaven. I came and asked her to do as I told her to do, but she refused to co-operate. So I beat her."

All laugh on hearing the story and say that he is really mad. Kabir comes forward and asks the others to leave, promising to take care of Tek Chand. After the others leave, Kabir speaks to him.

Kabir: "This is not the way to convert home into heaven. You have really done just the reverse and converted your home into a hell. That home in which the husband and wife quarrel is truly the worst hell. All peace disappears from there. You cannot expect to

101

have the least joy in the house where the husband and wife incessantly strike a discordant note. I find that you have not understood the philosophy behind what I demonstrated to you the other mornnng. It is not that by exactly repeating that process you can convert your home into heaven. By an expenditure of a rupee worth of *ghee* if a man can obtain heaven, then don't you think that all the people on earth would convert their homes into heavens? It is not so.

"The idea underlying what you saw is this. A wife should always be obedient to her husband. This again does not mean doing things unwillingly as a penance for having married the man. All that she does should be done whole-heartedly and with reverence, faith and devotion. This she will do if you win her heart by inspiring confidence in her, by convincing her of your good intentions and satisfying her wants even before she expresses them. You must read her heart, understand her temperament, behave nicely and with affection towards her and win her love. This will induce your wife to obey you implicitly and without the necessity of your having to apply force. The house in which the husband and wife lead such a life is without doubt heaven itself.

29

HYPOCRITICAL PREACHER

PUNDIT RAM SASTRI was a very learned man;
He lived in Coimbatore;
He used to give wonderful discourses;
He as a Shad-Darshan Sastri;
He knew the *Gita, Upanishads* and *Brahma Sutras.*
One day he chanted Pushpanjali—
Ta Karmana Ta Prahaya Dhanena
Tyagenaike Amritattvam Aanasuh—
"Not by works, nor by children, nor by wealth,
But by renunciation alone man attains immortality."
When he chanted this, all the people laughed heartily,
Because he himself was not living the divine life;
He had married a third woman;
He did not have a bit of renunciation;
He clung to his young wives.
Mere interpretation and recitation are of no avail;
What is wanted is actual, practical life.
Be practical and attain Self-realisation.

KANJANI

AT THE FOOT OF the Gandhamadana mountain there lived an old woman. She loved seclusion. She was the worst of all misers in the country. She lived alone because in the company of others she would have to share some of her possessions. Charity was unknown to her. She did not part with even a grain of rice or wheat during her lifetime.

Lord Vishnu watched with interest the life and actions of this famous old lady. He found that she was to die soon. She had only three more days of her life on earth.

The Lord therefore called Kaka Bhusandi to His side and said, "O My dear Bhusandi! look at this old lady. She has not done even a little of charity. She has been miserly all throughout her life. You go and try to snatch something from her at least today, because tomorrow she has to die. When she dies she will have some merit to her credit."

Kaka Bhusandi nodded assent. He took the form of a crow and sat on a tree near the house of Kanjani. It was the time when she was washing a handful of black gram soaked in water for cooking her food. Bhusandi decided to snatch away a beakful of gram.

Suddenly, at one leap he flew near the vessel and took a beakful of grain with lightning speed. The alert Kanjani grabbed him with greater speed. She wrung his neck and kept it twisted lest the grain slip down into his stomach. Meanwhile, with her other hand, she parted the beak and took out the gram to the last grain from the throat of the struggling crow.

Kaka Bhusandi struggled for his life. At last he was let free. He flew to Lord Vishnu and fell at His feet. Lord Vishnu questioned him as to what had happened after he left Him. Bhusandi gasped out the whole story and said, "O Lord! I was almost strangled to death. I could not succeed in my mission. I could not get even a grain of food from that wretched old lady."

Then the Lord said, "O Bhusandi! do not say so. Come, let Me examine your mouth."

Bhusandi opened his mouth. Lord Vishnu noticed a small bit of gram husk sticking to his palate, and said, "Look Bhusandi! there is a small bit of husk sticking to your palate. I am satisfied. The old lady has earned something. When she goes back to the world after death, let her be fed on the husk of the particular gram which is found sticking to your palate."

So saying, the Lord disappeared.

Great and marvellous are the benefits of charity and righteousness. Infinite and overwhelming is the love and compassion of the Lord. Such is the mysterious potency of even the least act of kindness and charity, that the fruit of it will cling to you and save you in your life beyond. The Lord Himself, in His great love, creates opportunities for the redemption and deification of the sinning man. Man has to grasp such opportunities as veritably God-sent.

When the old woman, who did no meritorious act,

was ordained to get bread made of husk, what will be the result of your hundreds of meritorious acts of poor-feeding, clothing the naked, relieving the distress of others, and comforting the sorrowful? One bit of husk will multiply itself a thousand-fold and feed the old lady in her next life. Such is the glory of charity and Dharma! Dharma, even though insignificant and minute, if practised with devotion, brings a hundred-fold beneficial results.

Therefore, friends, practise Dharma. Give up unrighteous conduct and way of life. Give up cruelty and hatred. Soar high into the realms of peace and bliss. Be good and do good. Let your life be simple and dignified. Work for the good and welfare of others. Share what you have with all. This will fill your life with peace and plenty. This is the ideal life that one should strive to lead.

May you all become embodiments of charity and generosity! May you all attain blessedness through charity!

THE WISE MONGOOSE

AFTER THE FAMOUS Mahabharata war was over, and after the death of Bhishma, Yudhisthira was very much afflicted at heart because of the slaughter of his kinsmen and others. He wanted to abandon his kingdom and retire to the forest.

Lord Krishna and Vyasa advised him to perform a sacrifice called the "Aswamedha Yajna". It was regarded as a great purifier of sins.

Yudhisthira performed the sacrifice on a grand scale. All the people, including the Brahmanas, praised the sacrifice.

While the Brahmanas were singing the praises of Yudhisthira's sacrifice, a mongoose appeared on the scene before them and said, "This sacrifice is not worth as much as the barley meal gift made by the liberal Brahmana of Kurukshetra, who was observing the Unchcha vow."

The Brahmanas were struck with wonder. They requested the mongoose to give its explanation.

The mongoose said, "I shall narrate a story to all of you. I shall tell you of the excellent fruit acquired by a Brahmana, who made a gift of a little measure of powdered barley that he earned by noble

"In the holy land of Kurukshetra, there lived a Brahmana who was observing the Unchcha vow. That mode of living is like that of the pigeon. He earned his livelihood by gleaning grains from the harvested fields. He lived with his wife, son and daughter-in-law and practised penances. The family generally ate a meal once in six days. If they did not get a meal on the sixth day, they ate on the twelfth, and if they did not get one on the twelfth, they ate on the eighteenth.

"Once there was a famine in the country. As they were about to sit down to partake of their meals, there appeared a guest. The Brahmana paid due respect. He gave the guest a portion of the barley meal that he was about to eat.

"The guest ate it but his hunger was not appeased. The wife of the Brahmana then offered her share. Her husband told her, 'Even among insects, worms and beasts the females are nourished with care. I will lose my honour if I let your share be given away. You are already lean. There is only skin and bone in your body. I will give the remainder of my share to the guest and satisfy his hunger.'

"But the wife insisted on giving her share to the guest and did so. The guest ate it but he still continued to be hungry.

"The Brahmana, his son and daughter-in-law then gave their share in turn one by one. Now the guest was perfectly satisfied. He said, 'I am highly pleased with this pure gift of yours, this gift of what was acquired by honest means by you and with which you parted freely according to the rules of virtue.'

"The guest went on, 'With this gift of powdered barley you have conquered the eternal region of Brahman. O foremost of the twice-born! a celestial car is here for all of you. It has come from heaven, attended by the Devas and Apsaras. Kindly get into the car and go to the celestial region. O Brahmana! I am the Deity of righteousness. Behold me!'

"Thereupon the Brahmana with his wife, son and daughter-in-law proceeded to the celestial region."

The mongoose further added, "I came out of the hole and found a little remnant of the barley flour on the ground at the spot. I rolled over it and found as a result that my head and one side of my body which had come into contact with the particles of that flour had become golden. I wanted to make the other half of the body also golden. I went to various places where great sacrifices had taken place and rolled at such places, but to no effect. They had not as much merit as the barley meal gift. I expected that the golden line of my body would be complete at the sacrifice of Yudhisthira, but the colour of my body has not been changed here. This clearly shows that there is not as much merit in this sacrifice as the self-sacrificing barley meal gift made by the poor Brahmana and his family."

Wealth and grandeur are not the real criteria for judging the value of a sacrifice. The Brahmana and his family made the greatest sacrifice with the gift of a little barley flour alone. They made the noblest and loftiest self-sacrifice.

32

IBRAHIM ADAHM

IBRAHIM ADAHM, a great Sufi, used to travel with pomp and splendour and with a large retinue of servants. His tents were pitched with golden pegs.

One day a wandering Dervish happened to pass by his tents and was greatly surprised to learn that all the things of luxury were owned by one who was once a king and now a Sufi. With a begging-cup in his hand the Dervish approached the kingly Sufi and said, "It is strange that you call yourself a Sufi and still own so much of worldly goods and your tents are fixed with golden pegs."

Ibrahim bade the Dervish have a little rest. After an hour or so he invited him to travel to Mecca in his company. The Dervish agreed.

The princely Sufi started on the pilgrimage with the Dervish, leaving all his tents and retinue behind. Both of them had not gone far when the Dervish remembered that he had forgotten his wooden cup in the tent and requested Ibrahim to allow him to go back to fetch it.

The Sufi then remarked, "This is just the difference between us two—I could afford to part with all my valuables without the least mental worry, while you could not part with a cup of practically no value without inconvenience. The golden pegs which so much surprised you were driven in the earth and not in my heart."

Ignorant and worldly-minded people judge others from their outward actions. In fact, it is the mental attitude that is the real action. Even though the ordinary worldly person and the sage do one and the same action, the former is bound by such action since he is doing it out of base desires, egoism and attachment, whereas the latter is not, as he is free from egoism and all sorts of attachments.

The sage who is full of wisdom and renunciation, who is devoted to the Lord, is above all formalities. Though he is wise, he plays like a child; though he is skilled in everything, he behaves like a simpleton; though he is a man of erudition, he talks like an ordinary man, without thirsting for applause or name and fame. He eats the food, rich or poor, good or bad, which he gets by chance. He keeps the same state of mind when he gets comforts or when he is under privation. He is above the pairs of opposites, since he is one with the all-pervading Brahman. The deluded one, on the other hand, is elated when he gets the objects of desire and easily grieved when he fails to get his desired objects.

33

DURYODHANA AND YUDHISTHIRA

ON ONE OCCASION the disciples of Dronacharya asked their Guru, "How is it, adorable Lord, that Yudhisthira is recognised as an embodiment of virtue and Duryodhana as a wicked man?"

Dronacharya demonstrated to his disciples that the reputation enjoyed by the two cousins was not without foundation. He called Duryodhana and said to him, "O Duryodhana! find out a virtuous man."

Duryodhana travelled far and wide and came back after a long time. He said to Dronacharya, "My adorable Guru, I could not find even a single virtuous man in the whole world. I saw men of evil nature everywhere."

Dronacharya then said to Yudhisthira, "O King! find out and bring a wicked man to me."

Yudhisthira also travelled far and wide and came back after a long time. He said to Dronacharya, "My worthy Master, I could not find even a single wicked man."

Thus the reports of the two princes were of a conflicting nature. All the disciples of Dronacharya were surprised at these two contradictory reports and could not make out which was correct.

Duryodhana and Yudhisthira

Dronacharya then said, "One sees one's own mind reflected in the world. Hence the whole world appears to be full of virtuous men to Yudhisthira and abounding in evil to Duryodhana. He who suffers from jaundice sees the whole world tinged with yellow colour. As is the mind, so is the vision."

34

MENTAL WORSHIP

MANASIC PUJA is mental worship. The devotee does not use external objects of worship such as flowers, etc., in this kind of worship.

Arjuna was very fond of doing long and ostentatious external worship of God. He had a spacious worship room lit up with countless lights. He used gold and silver vessels. He spent several hours in ceremonial worship of Lord Siva. He would sit for many hours and throw cartloads of flowers at the image of Lord Siva.

Bhima, the brother of Arjuna, never sat to do any worship. He never went to the temple. He used to close his eyes for a few minutes just before dinner and do mental worship of Lord Siva.

Arjuna thought that he was a great devotee of the Lord and that he was highly pious and devoted. He thought that his brother had no devotion and looked upon him with contempt.

Lord Krishna found out the attitude of Arjuna and wanted to teach him a good lesson and bring him to his senses. He proposed to Arjuna a trip to Mount Kailas, the abode of Lord Siva.

Arjuna did not suspect anything. He gladly consented to the proposal of Sri Krishna. They both started on the journey. On their way they met a man dragging a cart loaded with flowers of diverse kinds. Arjuna asked the man where he was taking the flowers to, but the man kept silent as he was very much absorbed in his work.

Lord Krishna said, "Arjuna, let us follow the man and find out the thing for ourselves."

Arjuna agreed and they both followed the man. They saw him empty the cart by the side of a huge heap of flowers which was as big as a hill. They further saw several hundreds of carts all loaded with flowers approaching the same spot and emptying their contents there.

Arjuna became more and more curious. He could not control his curiosity anymore. He asked the men, "Please tell me where these carts come from."

None of them replied, but one man said after repeated questioning, "Venerable sir, kindly do not disturb us. We are busy with our work. We have no time to talk to anybody. We have brought only seven hundred and fifty carts of flowers and more than seven hundred and fifty are still in the temple. They are all the flowers with which one, Bhima, a son of Pandu, worshipped our Lord yesterday. Now it is hardly four more hours before his worship today and we must remove all the flowers within that time."

Arjuna was struck with wonder. He asked, "Is it Bhima or Arjuna that you speak of, my friend? I think you are making a mistake."

The man replied, "Pooh! Arjuna! Not at all. It is Bhima who does such glorious worship with intense devotion and not his brother Arjuna, who merely makes an outward show of his worship."

Just then another man came with a basket of

115

flowers. Lord Krishna asked that man, "Friend, whose offerings are these?"

The man replied, "They were offered yesterday by an ostentatious man who lives on the earth. He is known as Arjuna and he makes a display of his worship without any real love and devotion."

Arjuna hung his head in shame and said to the Lord, "O Krishna! why did you bring me here? Let us leave this place at once. You could have pointed out my defects, my self-conceit and ostentation at home and saved all this trouble and exertion. I do admit that I thought very highly of my worship and devotion. I treated Bhima with contempt. I now realise that Bhima's short meditation with sincere devotion is more valuable and potent than all my showy worship."

Lord Krishna smiled and remained silent.

Though mental worship is more powerful than external worship, beginners should not leave the external form of worship. They should not at once start with Manasic Puja and disregard external worship. Many Nayanar saints attained Siva-Sayujya through external worship done with intense and sincere devotion. Those who are advanced on the path of devotion can do mental worship exclusively.

35

THE MAGIC SEAT

ONCE THERE LIVED an old man at the foot of the Vindhya Hills. His name was Vittal Jadhao. He was very poor and possessed nothing but a thatched hut. He was very lazy and therefore had to suffer much in life.

Vittal Jadhao had heard that Sadhus possessed Siddhis or Yogic powers which could create many things according to their wishes. One day, as he was thinking of a plan to live without doing any work, this fact came to his mind forcibly and he thought that if he could go to the caves of the Vindhya Hills he would surely meet a Sadhu and get from him what he wanted. With this intention he started for the caves.

After walking a considerable distance he met a Sadhu. He went to him and prostrated. The Sadhu entertained him nicely and enquired about the purpose of his visit.

Vittal Jadhao said, "Beloved Guruji, I am a very poor man. Except for a small hut I possess nothing. In this old age I am also unable to work and earn something. Kindly help me by giving me some wealth. I know perfectly well that you can at once produce as much money as you like through your Yogic powers."

The Yogi kept silent. The old man pressed him again

117

and again with his request. The Sadhu at last gave him a seat, saying that whenever he wanted something he should sit on the seat after washing his hands, feet and face, and think of the thing he wished to have. Whatever thought entered his mind would at once materialise. Thus he could obtain anything without effort.

The old man thanked the Sadhu heartily and, taking the seat, proceeded swiftly to his house. He did not want to waste any time and at once washed his face and sat on the seat. As he felt very hungry he thought of food first. Immediately a most sumptuous meal of various tasty dishes appeared before him. He ate to his heart's content. Then he wanted to have a rest and so he thought of a bed. He got a bed with a spring mattress and silken pillows. He rested for a while but his mind was as restless as ever.

He rose from his bed and again sat on the seat. He now wanted his hut to be changed into a big palace. Within the twinkling of an eye the old, thatched hut turned into a beautiful palace. On beholding the palace he rejoiced very much. Yet he thought that such a big palace would be of no use without a large amount of wealth. Immediately bags of gold, silver and diamonds were placed at his feet. Now the joy of the old man knew no bounds. But he wanted some servants to attend on him. They also came and stood with folded hands in front of him.

The old man rejoiced very much, but lo! the thought occurred to him that if there should be an earthquake what would be his position. Suddenly an earthquake demolished his palace to the ground and the old man and his servants perished in the ruins.

Desire is a great obstacle, a great barrier on the path

118

The Magic Seat

to Self-realisation. Control of mind really means abandoning desires. If one wants to discipline the mind perfectly one must give up all desires without reserve. All longing for worldly objects and building castles in the air must be abandoned. The monkey-mind is always restless, desiring something or other. Just as the fish taken out of the water tries to get into the water by some means or other, so also the mind will always be restless and will entertain evil thoughts. By killing all desires ruthlessly, by controlling the mind and emotions one can attain one-pointedness.

The mind has to be freed frcm all the surging emotions and bubbling thoughts before one can attain concentration. Such a mind will be as calm as a lamp in a windless place. One who attains such a state of mind will be able to meditate for a long time. Meditation will come by itself.

If one allows the mind to run towards worldly things according to its own wish, and to entertain unholy thoughts and evil desires, one will surely meet with destruction in the end.

Therefore, give up desires. Always have the one idea to attain to the Supreme Being, the abode of all joy, peace, bliss and immortality. Practise real Sadhana. Be regular in your Yogic practices. Strive to attain the goal of life in this very birth. You will then rejoice for ever.

36

GURU BHAKTI

THERE WAS ONCE a man of good spiritual impressions who used to attend Satsang classes where he heard that the Guru's Grace was indispensably necessary for God-realisation. From that very moment he began to search for a Guru to receive instructions and practise Sadhana. He came across many Sadhus and saints but found some fault or other with every one of them. He had a perverted intellect and a narrow-minded, fault-finding nature. Therefore he was not able to find a Guru. As long as one does not crush one's pride of intellect and learning and become like a child with intense faith, one cannot find a suitable Guru.

One day, while sitting in his house in a sorrowful mood, his wife asked him the reason for his lamentation. He replied that he could not find a Guru who would show him the way to God. His wife suggested that they should both go to the forest at night and sit on the wayside, and the man who happened to pass that way first should be taken as their Guru. The husband agreed.

The next day they went to the jungle and sat on the side of a pathway. It so happened that a thief with

some stolen ornaments was hurrying that way. The
couple at once caught hold of his feet and took him as
their Guru. They begged him to teach them the Guru
Mantra.

The thief was very surprised and also frightened.
They narrated the whole story to him. He was moved
by their faith and expressed the truth that he was a
thief. The couple, however, would not allow him to go
further and insisted that he teach them the Guru
Mantra. The thief was alarmed that if he tarried any
longer he would be caught. In order to get away
somehow, he asked them to bend down, close their
eyes and catch hold of their ears. He asked them to
remain in that posture until he again ordered them to
stand. They obeyed him and assumed the position.
They remained like that throughout the night and the
next day also. The couple did not take any food or
water. In the meantime the thief was caught and put
into prison.

Lord Vishnu and Goddess Lakshmi were very much
moved by their faith. Lakshmi became restless and
prayed to the Lord to give them Darshan. Lord Vishnu
appeared before them.

On seeing the Lord the couple were pleased but did
not open their eyes or stand up. The Lord requested
them to stand up but they replied that they would not
do so without the permission of their Guru.

Thereupon the Lord appeared before the ruler of the
country in a dream and asked him to release the thief
from prison. The Rajah thought that the dream was
false, but when it was repeated thrice, he at once
released the thief. The same night the Lord appeared
in the dream of the thief and told him to go to the
place where the couple still remained in the same

posture as he had ordered, and ask them to open their eyes.

Upon his release the thief immediately proceeded to the jungle and asked the couple to open their eyes and stand up. They did so and explained how the Lord had given them Darshan. The thief too revealed to them his dream and about his release.

A voice from heaven was heard: "I am very much pleased with the intense faith you have in your Guru. Do Bhajan, Japa and meditation regularly. I will give you Darshan and liberate you from the cycle of births and deaths."

From that day onward the thief also left his habit of stealing and became a devotee of Lord Vishnu. The couple commenced regular Sadhana and Bhajan and became liberated souls while living.

Devotion and obedience to the Guru can achieve anything. Guru Bhakti is the supreme purifier and illuminator. It is devotion to the Guru alone that makes the life of the aspirant blessed and fruitful.

37

THE JACKAL AND THE VULTURE

THIS INCIDENT happened in the Maimisha forest. A Brahmin who had been without children for a long time obtained a son after much penance. The child, however, died of infantile convulsion. The parents were plunged in grief. They carried the body to the burial ground. There also they lamented much.

Hearing their cries, a vulture came there and said, "See, the whole world is subject to happiness and misery. Union and disunion are seen in turns. Those who come to the crematorium with the dead bodies of their relatives, and those who sit by these bodies, themselves depart from the world due to their own acts, when the allotted periods of their lives expire. Whether friends or enemies, no one comes to life after having yielded to the power of time. Such indeed is the destiny of all creatures. In the world of mortals everyone who is born is sure to die. Who shall restore life to one who is dead and gone on the way ordained by the destroyer? Go home, renouncing the love for the child."

Hearing these words of the vulture the grief of the parents lessened a bit. They took the advice of the vulture and turned back home.

At this juncture a jackal came out of his hole and said to the parents, "Have you no affection for the child? The sun still shines in the sky. Give vent to your feelings fearlessly. The child may yet regain its life. Why do you want to go away with hearts of steel, renouncing every affection for the darling? Surely you have love for that child. Mark the affection that even birds and beasts cherish for their young ones. Shed tears for him for some time and look at him with affection a little longer. Life is dear to all and all feel the influence of love."

The speech of the jackal changed the minds of the parents and they decided to stay with the child a little longer.

The vulture again came out and said, "Why do you turn back at the call of a cruel, mean and dull-witted jackal? Why do you lament for that compound of five elements, deserted by the presiding gods, no longer occupied by the soul, motionless and stiff as a log of wood? Why do you not grieve for yourselves? Do you practise austerities by means of which you will succeed in purifying yourselves from sin? Anything can be obtained through penances. What will your lamentations do? Practise penance and get a long-living child. Death is born with the body. Wealth, wine, gold, precious gems, children—all these originate from penances. Penances again are the outcome of Yoga. The son is not fettered by the actions of the father or the father by those of the son. Fettered by their own actions, good and bad, all have to wend this common road. Of what use is mourning? Why do you grieve for the dead? Time is the master of all and by its very nature it looks impartially on all things. In proud youth or in helpless infancy, in old age or while lying

The Jackal and the Vulture

in the mother's womb, everyone is subjected to death. Such is the nature of the world."

The jackal said, "One should exert. Exertion and destiny joining together, yield fruits. Why then do you return so heartlessly? Stay here till the sun sets."

Once again the vulture spoke, "I am a thousand years old this day, but I have never seen a creature revive after death. The extent of life is fixed beforehand. Leave this dead body of the child, which has no animal heat and whose life will enter a new body."

Having heard these words of the vulture, the mourners resolved to leave the place.

Just as they were about to leave, the jackal came out quickly and said, "Rama, a dead Brahmana child was restored to life. The son of the royal sage, Sheweta, died prematurely, but the virtuous king succeeded in reviving his dead child. Similarly, in your case also, some Siddha, Muni or Devata may be willing to grant your desire and show mercy to you who are crying piteously for your child."

The mother placed the head of the child on her lap and they all wept again.

The jackal and the vulture both spoke repeatedly, answering each other's arguments. Both of them based their arguments on the scriptures. The vulture frightened the parents by talking of the wild beasts, goblins and other beings who would infest the place as soon as darkness set in.

Mother Parvati took pity on the parents and prevailed upon Siva to restore the child to life. Lord Siva granted life to the dead child, extending it to a hundred years. The parents were surprised to find life returning to the body. They returned to their home

125

happily. They glorified Lord Siva and worshipped Him.

The jackal really wanted the parents to stay till sunset so that he could eat the flesh without it being claimed by the vulture. The vulture wanted them to go away so that he could eat the body before sunset. Both of them were disappointed when life came back to the child. Both were miserable.

In this world the vast majority are selfish like the jackal and the vulture. They give good counsel to others but with selfish motives. They have their own axe to grind. Do not be duped by being over credulous. Use your own judgment. Be cautious. Think well.

126

A SON-IN-LAW

RAJENDRA WAS a religious-minded boy. He was in the habit of taking various sorts of vows in order to control the mind and the senses.

One day he went to his mother-in-law's house for Deepavali for the first time. On that day, Leelavathi, his mother-in-law, prepared very fine soup with fish for her son-in-law. Rajendra sat down to take his dinner. He was observing a vow of not leaving anything on his plate after his meals and also of not talking during meals.

Leelavathi served him with delicious rice, *dhal* and fish soup. Rajendra did not at all like fish. What was he to do now? He was observing the vow of silence; he could not say that he did not like the fish. He could not leave anything on the plate either. Somehow he swallowed the whole lot with great difficulty. The mother-in-law again served him with another lot of fish. She wanted to please him to her satisfaction. She thought that he liked fish very much. Rajendra swallowed the second lot also with added difficulty.

As soon as the plate became empty, Leelavathi served him again with a further lot. She thought within herself: "How happy I am! My son-in-law has almost finished all the soup. I am sure he likes my preparation very much. He does not even leave the bones but gulps down the whole mass with avidity."

Rajendra polished off this lot also!

Again the mother-in-law placed another big cupful of fish soup on the plate. Rajendra's stomach was about to burst! He could not take even a single drop of soup any more. He was forced to speak now and leave the soup on the plate.

He said to his mother-in-law, "My dear mother-in-law, I do not like fish at all. As I took the vow of keeping silent and not leaving anything on my plate, I was forced to swallow whatever you served. You thought that I liked the soup very much. You made a serious mistake. I also made a terrible mistake. My stomach is aching now. I have swallowed the bones also. Kindly send for the doctor immediately. The pain is becoming unbearable. My abdominal colic is very severe. I want to lie down immediately. Even if I wish to vomit there is no space inside to insert my fingers."

Leelavathi called for the doctor immediately. He came and slowly extracted the fish bones from the throat with long forceps. Rajendra was not able to move about or wash his hands. Two men had to carry him to the verandah and wash his hands. The doctor gave a strong emetic and did lavage of his stomach, gave an enema and an injection of morphine. Rajendra was relieved of the pain. He had to break all his vows.

Aspirants make serious mistakes. They should not take too many vows all at once. They should not go beyond their capacity and strength. They should move step by step on the spiritual path. They should observe one vow for a short time, and when they have gained sufficient strength they should prolong the period. They can take up another vow with caution.

Observe silence for a week. If you are able to keep the vow of silence for a week and if you do not experience any difficulty, then extend it for a fortnight, then for a month and afterwards for three months. If you take the vow all at once for three months, you may have to break it like our friend Rajendra. The object of any vow is to check the wandering mind and turbulent senses. Therefore use your intelligence and common sense always.

39

A SANNYASIN

SWAMI SATCHIDANANDA Saraswati, an aged monk,
was passing along a street in Madura. An arrogant and
mischievous merchant called the Swami and asked,
"O Swamiji! please tell me which is superior—your
beard or the tuft of hair on the tail of a donkey?"
   The Swami did not say a word.
   Five years rolled by. Swami Satchidananda was
dying of typhoid fever. He sent one of his disciples to
fetch the merchant, who appeared before him.
   The Swami said, "O merchant! now I can give you a
definite answer to your question. My beard is un-
doubtedly superior to the tuft of hair on the tail of a
donkey."
   The merchant asked, "O venerable Swamiji! why did
you not give me an answer then?"
   The Sannyasin replied, "Now that my Pranas are
about to depart from the body, there is no chance of
me doing a wrong action. There is no chance of me
having a downfall. Up to this time I have led a very
pure life, so I am quite sure of the purity of my life and
can therefore boldly state now that my beard is
superior to the tuft of hair on the tail of a donkey.
   "The life of a Sannyasin is beset with numerous

A Sannyasin

temptations. A Sannyasin may become very famous. He may have a hopeless downfall at any moment. His very disciples and admirers may forsake him and treat him with contempt and scorn. We cannot say anything definite regarding the character of a Sannyasin or any man till the last breath leaves his body. Maya is very powerful and mysterious. This world is full of all kinds of temptations. Even an advanced aspirant may fall if he is careless, if his dispassion wanes or if he is not regular in his meditation. Have you not heard the story of Viswamitra? He fell a victim to the celestial nymph despite his rigorous austerities."

The arrogant merchant was struck with wonder when he heard the wise words of the Swami. He prostrated before him and apologised for his indecent and rude question.

40

A PRACTICAL VEDANTIN

RADHAKRISHNA HAD read a few books on Vedanta such as *Vichar Sagar, Panchadasi* and *Atma Bodha.* He thought within himself that he was a great Vedantin and a realised soul. He never studied the books under a Guru and did not get any initiation either. The practice of meditation and contemplation was unknown to him.

One day Radhakrishna went to a shop for a cup of milk. While drinking the milk he was philosophising within himself: "There is only one Self everywhere. I have also read: 'Everything is mine, all is mine, all is Brahman.' So let me become a practical Vedantin now."

The shopkeeper had to go to a neighbouring shop to purchase some sugar. The box in which the money was kept was open. He had forgotten to lock it up.

Radhakrishna quietly took out a one hundred rupee note from the box and walked away silently down the street. He thought within himself: "This money-box is mine, this money is mine, everything is mine. Today I have realised the right significance of Vedanta. How practical Vedanta is! How beautiful it is to live in the true spirit of Vedanta! How happy I am! The wealth of

A Practical Vedantin

the whole world is mine now. Everything is mine."

The shopkeeper returned and found the money-box open. He counted the money and found that a hundred rupee note was missing. He immediately ran down the street and caught hold of Radhakrishna and handed him over to the police inspector.

Radhakrishna appeared before the district magistrate for trial.

The magistrate asked, "Radhakrishna, did you take the one hundred rupee note from the box of the shopkeeper?"

Radhakrishna replied, "Yes, my Lordship, I took it from the box."

The magistrate asked, "Why did you take it?"

Radhakrishna replied, "I wanted to practise and feel Vedanta in daily life. I desired to live in the spirit of Vedanta. I have read the Vedantic books which state: 'Everything is mine, all is mine.' So I thought that the money in the box was mine and took it. I have not stolen the money. I am not a thief."

"Very beautiful Vedanta indeed!" replied the magistrate. "The world is really in dire need of such Vedantins. Then only will the misery of the world come to an end.

"Well, Radhakrishna, listen to the other part of Vedanta. It says: 'I am not the body, I am the Self.' Let me see how far you have conquered attachment to the body and whether you have really gone above body-consciousness."

The magistrate asked the police constable to thrash him severely with a whip.

Radhakrishna cried out bitterly and said, "O my Lordship! I have not put this part of Vedanta into practice. This is very difficult. I am only the body now.

133

Kindly request the police constable to cease beating me. I cannot bear the pain any longer. I will swoon shortly. I have realised my folly now. Vedanta is really very difficult to practise. I have come to my senses. I will not commit such foolish acts in the future."

The magistrate said, "Radhakrishna, go to a Brahmanishta Brahmashrotri Guru. Live with him for twelve years. Serve him with devotion. Study the *Vedas* under him carefully. Develop all the divine qualities. Hear, reflect, meditate and realise your true Self. Then only can you say, 'I am Brahman, all is mine'."

Radhakrishna obeyed the instructions of the magistrate. He proceeded to Rishikesh and found a Guru. He lived with him for a period of twelve years, practised rigorous austerities and meditation and eventually realised the Self.

These days, dry or lip-Vedantins are in abundance. There is much Vedantic gossiping. There are many Radhakrishnas. Mere talk on Vedanta, mere study of *Vichar Sagar* or *Panchadasi* cannot make one a practical Vedantin. Practical Vedantins are rare. You must have a correct and proper understanding of the scriptures and the words of the Guru. You have to remove the impurities and tossing of the mind. You have to tear the veil of ignorance. You have to struggle very hard. Rigorous Sadhana has to be done. The false identification with the body has to be conquered. The three Gunas, the five sheaths and the three states have to be transcended. Then you will rest in your own essential divine nature or Satchidananda state. Then only can one become a practical Vedantin or realised sage or Jivanmukta.

Glory to practical Vedantins who have realised their Atman! May their blessings be upon you all!

41

THE WISE LADY

A RELIGIOUS-MINDED and charitable Maharaja arranged a big show. All kinds of things were exhibited for free distribution. Any man or woman could take anything he or she liked. The people of the whole city came to the show.

Some took rich clothes, some took jewels, some took many valuable books, some others carried away fresh fruit from Cashmere. All were satisfied.

There was one wise old lady, however, who did not take anything. She was dissatisfied.

The Dewan reported this to the Rajah. "The people of the city are all highly satisfied but there is an old lady who is not. She says that she does not want anything from the storehouse. She wants to see the Rajah in person."

The Rajah then went on the back of an elephant to see the old lady in person. The old lady said, "O Rajah! come down from the elephant. I want to speak to you about something very important."

The Rajah got down from his elephant. The old lady at once caught hold of the right hand of the Rajah and said, "O Rajah! thou art now mine. I do not want these little objects or toys from the storehouse. I want to possess you only. The whole wealth of the state belongs to me as you are now mine."

The Rajah was astonished at the wise words of the old lady. He kept her in his palace and looked after her very carefully till the end of her life. He regarded her as his own venerable mother.

By entertaining various desires you run after the objects. There is neither satisfaction nor contentment. You have become a beggar of beggars by becoming a slave of desires. If you renounce mundane desires and objects and possess the Supreme Lord of this universe, all your desires will be gratified. Just as the old lady who virtually came into possession of the wealth of the state by claiming the Rajah himself, so also all spiritual wealth will belong to you if you possess Him through meditation and devotion.

Lord Jesus has said, "Seek ye first the Kingdom of Heaven, then all else shall be added unto you."

THE RICH AND THE POOR

THERE ONCE lived a poor man but he was full of love. He was loved by others in return. He had his quiet hours of prayer and meditation, and when he spoke, a smile played on his lips. Sometimes, however, he wished that he was rich.

One day he went to a forest and there came across an old man. The old man said to him, "I shall give you money and make you rich on one condition."

"What is that condition?" asked the poor man.

"Give me your heart of love."

"How shall I live then?" asked the poor man.

The old man replied, "I have a stone heart. It is wonderfully constructed. I shall take out your heart and put in its place the heart of stone. It will beat like a real heart of flesh."

The poor man consented. So the old man laid a spell on him and when he recovered he found that he had parted with his heart of love and had a stone heart instead.

He returned home and found that money came to him without any difficulty. Whatever he touched was turned into gold. But he also found that he could no longer love God or man. He found that he spoke harshly and entertained thoughts of anger. Then he discerned the truth—that life without the love of God and man was not a blessing but a burden.

There are many men walking along the pathway of life with hearts of stone. Look around and see how many are chasing after worldly vanities—money, power, reputation, position, gold, the opposite sex and sensual enjoyments. They miss the loveliness of life.

Lord Yama, the God of Death, said to Nachiketas, "The way to the hereafter is not apparent to the rich man, who is foolish, deluded by wealth. 'This is the world', he thinks, 'there is no other'—thus he falls again and again under my sway."

Therefore, dear brothers, develop a soft and loving heart and walk in the path of love and kindness. You will attain the final beatitude of life. You will be a blessing to the world and a lamp unto others. You will radiate peace, joy and comfort to those filled with pain, sorrow and suffering.

43

SIVAJI'S PRIDE QUELLED

SIVAJI, THE greatest hero of Maharashtra,
Built a very large fortress;
Thousands of labourers were working.
Sivaji thought: "I am feeding all these labourers."
Vanity and pride slowly crept into his mind.
Samartha Ramdas, Guru of Sivaji, noticed this;
He wanted to teach Sivaji a lesson.
One day he came to the palace
And eulogised the monarch very much.
Ramdas said, "Sivaji, you are helping many labourers;
A very great work you are doing."
Sivaji had great exhilaration of spirit;
He replied, "Guru Maharaj, it is all thy Grace only."
Ramdas then said, "Sivaji, break this rock."
At once a frog came out and water poured forth.
Ramdas asked, "Sivaji, who fed the frog in the rock?"
Sivaji came to his senses;
He hung his head in shame;
He said, "Forgive me, O Lord! My pride is quelled;
In future I will not entertain such thoughts."

44

TWO BIRDS

ONCE TWO BIRDS lived with their little ones in the field of a peasant. Every morning and evening they went in search of food for their young ones.

One evening, when the birds returned with food, the young ones were very excited. They said to their parents, "The peasant has requested his relatives to cut the crops tomorrow."

The parents replied, "My dear ones, do not be troubled at heart. His relatives will never help him to cut the crops. We are safe. Be cheerful."

The next day also the little birds said, "The peasant has requested his sons to help him to cut the crops."

The wise parents laughed and said, "My beloved ones, even now we are quite safe. You need not be unnecessarily alarmed. His sons will never help him."

On the third day the young birds reported, "The peasant has resolutely determined to cut the crops himself tomorrow. He said that he would not rely on anyone else."

The parent birds said, "Now it is very dangerous. We must move immediately to another field. The peasant will surely come to reap the crops as he is relying on himself only and not on others."

Two Birds

The birds moved at once with their little ones to another field. And, sure enough, the peasant did come himself the next day and cut the crops.

Self-reliance is the best of all virtues. Rely on your own self.

141

45

BE COURAGEOUS

PREM DEVI and her little son, Raghuvir, had abandoned their ancestral home where a disembodied spirit had taken a heavy toll of the lives of all their kith and kin. Prem Devi's parents and six brothers had all perished at the hands of the devil. She then decided that the best thing would be to abandon the house and go elsewhere to eke out a living.

A few years later, when the boy had grown into a young man, he one day asked his mother, "Mother, what place do we come from? My friends are asking me about this. They say we have run away from our ancestral home. Is that so, mother?"

"Yes, it is true, son."

"Why did you run away from there, mother?"

"Eight people had died in the house in the course of a month. It is not good to live in such a house. It is haunted."

"What harm will befall us, mother, if other people had died in the house? Come, let us go back to our home."

At the insistence of her son, they both returned.

Fear had not left the mother's heart. Every day she used to set apart a portion of their food "for the ghost"

Be Courageous

Only after this was done would they take their meals. The young man was very curious to know what it meant.

His opportunity came. One day the mother had prepared a dish which the son liked most. He wanted to appropriate the share of the devil also. The mother would not permit it.

"Why, mother, for whom is that?"

"For the devil which has eaten all your uncles."

"What! do you feed the devil that has killed your brothers? Absurd! I will eat it myself."

"No, son. The devil might harm us too. Leave it alone."

That day Raghuvir kept a close watch. When the devil came for its meal, Raghuvir asked, "O devil! who are you?"

"Young man, I am the ghost of the third cousin of your grandfather. It was I who killed your grandfather and uncles, because they robbed me of my property and let me die as a pauper."

"What is your strength?"

"I am extremely powerful. I can kill all your uncles and grandparents just as you kill bugs. I could have killed your mother too, but she escaped. Now she is feeding me, so I won't harm you. And listen—I can fly in a moment to the region of the gods and devils."

"Will you do me a favour? Can you take me to the region of the gods?" asked the boy.

"No, I can't do that."

"All right. Then take a message from me to the gods."

"I shall. What is it?"

"Ask the gods there how long I will live on this earth."

"Very good," said the devil and departed.

The very next day it brought the information.

"Raghuvir, you will live to be sixty."

"Another small favour, friend. Kindly ask the gods if they can make me die at fifty, or, if that is not possible, then let them make me live up to a hundred years."

"Right!" said the devil and went away.

"I conveyed your request to the gods," said the devil the next morning. "It is impossible either to extend your life-span or to shorten it even by a single day. What is ordained has to take place at the right time."

Raghuvir had anticipated this reply and had eaten the delicacies reserved for the devil. The moment this reply was given he took a burning log of wood from the kitchen and belaboured the devil severely.

"Get out of the house and return no more!"

He silenced his wailing mother, saying, "What can this devil do to me, mother? It cannot kill me a day earlier, nor can it do me more harm than my own Karma warrants. I will drive all the evil spirits out of this house. Take courage. We suffer not at the hands of our enemies, nor through insects and beasts, nor even from the wrath of ghosts and gods, but on account of our own past Karma and actions. We need be afraid of none but our own lower, passion-filled, erring selves. Take heart, mother! Let us adore God and lead the Divine Life. We shall have no fear of anything then."

46

BIRBAL AND HIS BROTHER-IN-LAW

BIRBAL WAS THE favourite minister of Akbar. He was famous for his wisdom and keen wit.

Birbal's brother-in-law, who was jealous of him, thought: "Why is the Badshah doting upon this man? I can manage the affairs of the state as efficiently as Birbal."

By using various crooked methods he approached the Badshah and advised him to dismiss Birbal.

"I can discharge the duties of the minister more efficiently and more loyally," he declared.

When Birbal heard of this, he smiled and thought of teaching his brother-in-law a lesson. He resigned his job, appointed the brother-in-law in his place and left the kingdom.

In order to test the efficiency of the new minister, Akbar gave him Rs. 500 and said, "I want you to spend this amount in such a manner that I will get Rs. 500 here on earth, Rs. 500 in the other world, Rs. 500 neither here nor there; and then you must return the Rs. 500 to me intact."

The new minister was greatly worried. He could not think of any way of achieving this. He spent sleepless nights. He did not relish his food and appeared anaemic within a few days. His wife advised him to approach Birbal. He had no other choice.

Birbal said to him, "Give me the money. I will do everything."

The new minister gave the Rs. 500 to Birbal. Birbal entered the kingdom and walked along the roads. A well known, wealthy businessman was celebrating the marriage of his daughter. Birbal entered the house and in the open pandal declared, "O merchant! Badshah has sent you this Rs. 500 as a wedding present. I have been deputed by him to make this present to you."

The merchant was immensely delighted. He entertained Birbal well and gave him many presents and large sums of money as his "return present" to the Badshah.

Birbal went to a nearby village. He bought foodstuff and sweets for Rs. 500 and distributed them to the poor in the name of the Badshah. He came back to the town and held a nautch party. He invited all the dancers and musicians and spent Rs. 500 on the entertainment.

Birbal then entered the Durbar of Akbar. Akbar was greatly pleased that Birbal had returned.

"Badshah Saheb, here is the Rs. 500. I have done all that you had asked my brother-in-law to do."

"How?" asked the Badshah.

"Rs. 500 I gave as your present to the merchant—that is for *here*. Rs. 500 I distributed among the poor—you will get it *there*, in the other world. Rs. 500 I spent on a nautch party—you will get it neither *here* nor *there*. And here is Rs. 500 as commanded by you."

Birbal's brother-in-law hung his head in shame. He was utterly humiliated. His jealousy vanished.

The story has another moral: the money that you

Birbal and his Brother-in-law

spend on your friends, you will get back here in the shape of service and help from them; the money that you spend in charity you will get in heaven in the shape of the Lord's richest blessings and a glorious life in the other world; the money you spend in sensual enjoyment is a mere waste and will help you neither here nor there. Therefore, do charity and enjoy everlasting happiness.

47

THE REWARD OF INSULT

DAYASINDHU WAS dancing along the roads of Puri. He felt hungry. He used to take only a glass of milk each day. Except this inevitable time spent in begging for milk, he was always immersed in the love of Jaganatha, in singing His Names and glories, in dancing and making others dance in joy and ecstasy.

A young woman was scrubbing the verandah of a nearby house. Dayasindhu went thither.

"Mother, give me a glass of milk. I am hungry."

That was the last straw! Waking up early in the morning, she had been going about her household duties, attending to the cows, bathing and dressing her half-a-dozen children and preparing breakfast for her husband. As she was scrubbing the floor now, one of her children was pulling at her hair, crying for sweets, another was suckling at her breast. She was obviously harassed on all sides. She exploded. Dayasindhu was the target.

"You wretched beggar! Get away! From early this morning I have been toiling hard for the sake of my husband and children. You lazy man, you have come to add to my miseries. Here, take this!" she said.

And instantly the dirt-laden, foul-smelling rag with

148

which she was scrubbing the floor flew towards Dayasindhu's face. She aimed at his face; the rag hit his chest.

Dayasindhu was beside himself with joy. "My Lord! what a marvellous thing you have given me this morning. Glory, glory to Thee!"

He altogether forgot about his quest for milk. He danced and sang his way to the sea. He washed the rag thoroughly, dried it, and made it into a suitable wick. He obtained a little *ghee* which he smeared on the wick.

Arati was in progress that evening in the temple of Jaganatha. Dayasindhu also joined the big crowd of devotees. He too had brought an offering unto the Lord—the rag-wick. Suddenly, to the astonishment of the assembled devotees, he lighted the wick and began waving it before the Lord. The people knew of Dayasindhu's supreme love for the Lord and so did not object. He was in ecstasy. People around him were singing His Names.

A young woman frantically rushed into the temple. Like a lunatic she ran inside, with dishevelled hair and her clothes sweeping the ground behind her.

"Hey Jaganatha! Hey Jaganatha! Hey Krishna!" she shouted. The moment she espied the presence of Dayasindhu, she leapt forward and fell prostrate at his feet. A shudder passed through her frame, an ecstatic smile lighted up Dayasindhu's face.

Little did the devotees who witnessed this entrancing spectacle know that this young woman had in a moment obtained the highest blessings of the Lord.

She had just finished cooking the evening meal and was taking her baby to the cradle. She did not lay it on the cradle but dropped it. She stared wildly in front of her and fell on her knees. The older children could not understand what had happened and cried in fright. She did not heed them. Streams of tears flowed down her cheeks. For a moment she was still, silent. In her heart shone the Light of the Lord. She saw Jaganatha in it, and she saw the beggar Dayasindhu waving the rag she had thrown at his face, now transformed into a torch of knowledge. She gave a wild cry: "Hey Prabho! Prananatha!"

Her husband, parents and neighbours gathered around but their faces had no meaning for her, nor was there on her face a look of recognition of her dear and near ones. She rushed out. No one dared to restrain her.

Not a word passed between the two. In the compassion-filled look of Dayasindhu's eyes, the lady read this message: "A Bhakta receives everything as His blessings. Whatever is offered to him is transferred to the Lord. He does not exist as separate from the Lord. He lives in the love of the Lord and for the service of the Lord. If you give him a cup of milk it will reach the Lord. If you throw a rag at his face, that too will reach the Lord. It will be joyously offered to Him. A Bhakta purifies and enlightens all who come into contact with him."

She became Dayasindhu's greatest disciple.

48

SECRET OF RIGHTEOUSNESS

LIFE CONSTANTLY imparts valuable lessons to every man. It instructs at every moment of your existence here on earth, but you are so heedless that you forget the lesson at once. Yet, without any disgust, Mother Prakriti again and again gives fresh lessons in the form of life's experiences. She is a tireless teacher and if you carefully retain the memory of the early experiences, you will never commit a mistake or stray away from the correct path. If you treasure these lessons and cherish the memory of the past experiences, you become wise and remain safe in your wisdom and in your greatness.

Dara was a humble shepherd in the land of Persia. He was of low birth and extremely poor, but was endowed with deep wisdom. He possessed shrewd insight and a great understanding concerning the nature of men and things.

The Shah of Persia, coming to know of Dara's wisdom and insight, took him into his service. Dara soon rose to the highest position as the Shah's chief councillor and trusted Prime Minister. This made the other nobles very jealous and they eagerly awaited a proper opportunity of bringing disgrace upon him and pulling him down from the high status that he occupied.

The Shah had unlimited confidence in Dara and once sent him as Governor designate to one of the most important provinces of his great kingdom. In his absence the hostile and jealous nobles reported many uncharitable things about Dara to the Shah. They accused him of corruption and told the Shah that he had amassed great riches by misappropriating royal revenue, and that he always took his ill-gotten treasure with him, closely secured in a chest. Wherever he went, this chest followed him on a camel's back, and he opened it only at night within the privacy of his own tent. He never once parted with the chest or ever opened it in public. This was the grave charge.

The Shah trusted Dara implicitly but the nobles insisted upon Dara being examined and exposed. At last the Shah paid a surprise visit to him and, entering his tent at night, said, "O Dara my faithful friend! pray show me the contents of that chest. I am curious to see what is in it."

Though he was reluctant, Dara obeyed the royal command, and before all slowly unlocked the chest, raising the lid and opening it fully. And lo! to the astonished gaze of the onlookers was revealed an old shepherd's cloak of plain, simple cloth, brown with dust and tattered with age. Except for this there was nothing else inside the chest—no gems, gold, silver, brass or even a single copper.

The mystified Shah directed inquiring eyes at the silent Dara and the latter explained: "Royal Shah, thou knowest now what I guarded closely all these years. This shepherd's garment I wore in the days before you found and favoured me with thy royal kindness. But position, prestige and power are dangerous things for the unwary man. They raise one high but pull one down into the dust as well. Prosperity and plenty, authority and respect, turn a man's head and take him away from the straight path. He alone is safe who constantly remembers who he was before fortune smiled upon him and God graced him. This alone reminds him of what he really is, and keeps him ever humble, righteous and true. Therefore I have retained this old cloak of mine to remind me of my former life. I look at it every night, lest I forget it in the intoxication of my present position and glory. This keeps me humble, true and simple. Royal Master, though outwardly Dara is thy chief councillor and a great Governor by thy favour, yet, even to this day, in reality, he is the same simple shepherd—humble, poor and incorruptible. And his one constant prayer to the Lord, His Divine Master, is that he may continue to be so."

O aspirants and seekers! learn this great lesson from the sagely Dara. Never forget what you really are in your heart of hearts. Do not let external changes and vicissitudes of fortune turn your head and make you plunge into delusion and unrighteousness. Cherish the lessons of life carefully, even as Dara treasured his humble cloak. Always remember life's lessons and thus remain unaffected by any passing phenomena. Just as Dara constantly remembered his shepherd origin, ever bear in mind your true Atmic origin. Do not be overcome by the influence of the impermanent secular egoism.

May the Lord bless you with an ever-alive enquiry into the nature of the Self and a constant awareness of your native, Atmic glory!

49

CHIPAK MAHADEV

IT WAS THE CUSTOM of a village in India that two months after marriage the bridegroom should visit the father-in-law's house, accompanied by a barber. This problem also faced the hero of this story. So a barber was sought. But the barber was very clever. He insisted that he accompany the bridegroom only on the condition that he be given to wear exactly the same kind of clothes as the bridegroom. This being agreed upon, both the bridegroom and the barber started.

When they neared the father-in-law's house, the clever barber asked the bridegroom to remain outside so that he could go and inform the family beforehand about his august arrival. The simple-natured bridegroom obeyed.

Now the cunning barber went into the house and told the mother-in-law that he had left the luggage outside along with a servant, and that the servant may be sent for. So the family took the bridegroom to be the servant and treated him as such, while the barber was treated like a prince. The poor bridegroom suffered in silence. This went on for quite some time.

One day it happened that there was no fuel in the house. The mother-in-law then asked the barber-

Chipak Mahadev

bridegroom if she could send his servant to the jungle to bring some firewood. The cunning barber quickly and willingly gave permission.

So the simple bridegroom went to the forest and collected some wood. As he had forgotten to take a rope along with him, he did not know what to do. Struck with sorrow he sat on the spot and began to weep over his fate.

Luckily for him, Lord Siva and Parvati passed that way, and Mother Parvati, when she saw him weeping, was filled with pity. She asked Lord Siva to enquire of the weeping man the cause of his sorrow. Lord Siva wanted to ignore the incident, but Mother Parvati insisted that the cause be found out. When Lord Siva asked the ill-fated bridegroom what made him weep, he related the whole story.

The Lord consoled the man and advised him that if he uttered the words "Chipak Mahadev", anything will stick in a marvellous manner. The poor bridegroom instantly tried the words on the wood, and all the sticks stuck together. He placed the bundle on his head and reached the house.

On his arrival he saw the barber taking milk. When he took the cup to his lips, the bridegroom quietly uttered the mysterious Mantra, "Chipak Mahadev". The cup instantly stuck to the lips of the barber! The barber was in an awkward condition. In the meantime, when the mother-in-law saw that he was not removing the cup from his lips, she was surprised and herself came to take the cup off. But as she placed her hand on the cup, the bridegroom again uttered the Mantra, "Chipak Mahadev". The poor woman remained where she was, unable to move her hand. One by one all the members of the family got caught in the trap and there

155

was a train of helpless victims all stuck together!

A Pundit who lived nearby was called. He came riding on a horse. Just as he alighted, he held the tail of the animal. Quietly the bridegroom repeated the same mystic words. The Pundit was wonderstruck. He just could not take his hands off the tail!

Now the Pundit reflected that all the members of the house were victims of this "sticking business" except one man. So he lovingly called the bridegroom and asked him what all this meant and how it was that he alone escaped from the punishment.

The good-natured bridegroom related the whole story. All were just wonderstruck and ashamed at treating the real bridegroom in such a disgraceful manner. The bridegroom then prayed to Lord Siva and everyone was released. The barber was given a nice thrashing which he well deserved. He was forthwith driven out of the house.

So the moral of the story is: do not cheat others.

50

STORY OF A KAUPEEN

ONCE A KAUPEEN (underwear) got disgusted with the position it was assigned on the wearer's body. It left him and went to Benares. There it was lying on the Ganges Ghat.

A Sadhu, who used to wear only a *kaupeen* on his person, and who had just then lost his only underwear in the current of the Ganges while taking a bath, chanced to notice this *kaupeen* lying on the Ghat.

Finding nobody in the vicinity who could possibly be its owner, the Sadhu took it and wore it, thus saving himself from the embarrassment of moving about in a state of nudity.

The poor *kaupeen* felt sorry that it had to cover the very same part of the Sadhu's person as it did in the body of the previous person. Hardly two or three days had passed when it realised that its new master was even more cruel than the previous one. The Sadhu, having no spare underwear, wore the new *kaupeen* all the twenty-four hours, whereas the previous owner wore it only on alternate days. The *kaupeen* mused within itself: "What a mistake I have committed! I ought not to have deserted my previous master. My new master does not give me a single day's rest."

Similarly, a buffalo too got disgusted with its hard work of ploughing its master's fields from morning till night. One night, while it was let loose for grazing, it ran off to a distant place. It was noticed by a farmer who, knowing that it had strayed away from its owner, made himself its new owner. He yoked it to the plough and made it work day and night.

The buffalo thought within itself: "Ah! what a blunder I have committed in running away from my previous master. He was indeed kind, for he never made me work at night, but my present master, cruel by nature, makes me work day and night and beats me mercilessly with his whip. I wish I had not deserted my previous master."

The *kaupeen* and the buffalo realised that none can escape playing his ordained role in the scheme of God, and any attempt to escape would prove futile and only land one into greater difficulties and forced fulfilment of the assigned role. The *kaupeen* and the buffalo now learnt that wisdom lay in meekly surrendering to the Divine Will and discharging one's allotted function, putting up with all the difficulties and inconveniences that one's duty involved.

One cannot expect ideal conditions to prevail anywhere, for the moment one gets such ideal conditions, the mind will still find some defects in those conditions and crave for still better conditions. It is a trick of the mind to escape discipline. A man of discipline puts up with all conditions, adjusts himself to all kinds of situations and discharges whatever duties are assigned to him. Though difficult, he discharges such duties with a happy and cheerful heart. Such a man of discipline is a true devotee of God.

True devotion is self-surrender. Devotion does not

158

consist so much in Japa, ecstatic Kirtan or elaborate ritual worship, as in surrendering oneself to the Divine Will and doing one's allotted work calmly, in a spirit of divine worship, without complaining of anything, accepting everything as sent by God for one's own quick evolution. The moment one adopts this attitude, every difficulty, every obstacle, becomes a help to march ahead on the path of evolution. To a true devotee who has surrendered himself to the Lord, no task is difficult, no task is mean, no work is an obstacle on the path of his spiritual progress, for he does everything knowing it to be worship of God and fulfilment of the Divine Will. He thus maintains God-consciousness at all times.

Yoga is essentially the maintenance of the state of God-consciousness at all times. It is not in Uttarkasi or Gangotri or in any place higher up in the Himalayas. It is in the right understanding that everything is God and all work is divine worship. Many aspirants leave the world and go to Rishikesh for seclusion. After a while they leave the place and search for seclusion higher up the Himalayas, at Uttarkasi or Gangotri. In the end they find it nowhere.

Even at Uttarkasi or Gangotri one has to go to others for alms. One has to create seclusion wherever one lives. Seclusion is impossible on this earth. Physical seclusion is useless if it is not combined with mental seclusion. Aspirants make no spiritual progress by moving about from place to place. It is like a rolling stone that gathers no moss. It spoils their health, and in the end, like the *kaupeen* and the buffalo, they realise their folly in leaving the place where God had placed them, in search of better ones.

Adapt, adjust and accommodate.

51

PRINCE NARENDRA

PRINCESS LILAVATHI, wife of Prince Narendra, used to worship Rama with great devotion. But Narendra never even uttered Ram-Nam. This pained Lilavathi much. She entreated her husband on many occasions to utter Ram-Nam, even if it was only once. Narendra was very obstinate. He refused to do so.

One morning Lilavathi was in great joy. She sent for the Diwan of the state and told him, "This is a day of great rejoicing for me. I will not tell you the reason now. Feed thousands of Brahmins and poor people. Let there be fireworks tonight. Let there be bands playing at all the gateways of the city.

The Diwan carried out the behests of the princess. There was great joy all over the city. Nobody knew why the show had been put up.

The prince witnessed all the rejoicing and asked the Diwan, "Diwan Sahib, what is the matter today?"

The Diwan replied, "I myself do not know the cause of the festivities. The princess ordered me to do all these things."

Then the prince asked his wife. She declined to tell him the cause but in the end had to yield to his repeated requests.

Prince Narendra

Princess Lilavathi said, "My dear, my heart is full today. My joy knows no bounds. I cannot adequately express my condition. I have obtained now what I wished for and which you declined to give in spite of my repeated entreaties.

"Last night in your sleep you uttered the Divine Name several times. This is quite sufficient for me. I am blessed now. This is a day of rejoicing for me and so I ordered the Diwan to arrange these festivities."

Narendra asked his wife, "What was the Name?"

Lilavathi replied, "Rama."

The prince exclaimed, "Ah! the treasure that I so long kept as a secret in the innermost recesses of my heart has at last come out!"

As the prince uttered these words he dropped down dead!

Lilavathi was dumbfounded. She had never known up to this time that her husband had been a silent, sincere and unassuming devotee of Rama.

A real devotee would never like to advertise his devotion and piety. It is only the hypocrite who makes much show of his devotion and displays his piety. He shouts, "Hari, Hari", wears several rosaries around his neck and sheds false, crocodile tears just to attract people and get some money. Credulous, ignorant people are deceived. But the hypocrites are found out in the end. A true devotee does not easily reveal himself. He never cares to make himself known. An empty vessel only makes much sound. The religious hypocrite deceives God and others. Centres of pilgrimage always abound in religious hypocrites. They are the real vultures of the place and feed on innocent pilgrims.

Never try to pose as a devotee or a pious man. Do not

161

let people know of your spiritual Sadhana. Do not make a show of Japa and meditation. Do it sincerely. You can wear a rosary around your neck underneath your shirt or upper cloth. Do not trumpet forth your spiritual experiences.

52

INFATUATED LOVE

MOHAN LOVED his wife Savitri passionately. Savitri was a very beautiful woman. She had great devotion to the Lord and had studied Vedantic literature also. She was endowed with discrimination and dispassion and practised meditation daily.

One day, Mohan told Savitri that it was his prayer that after their death he may forever be in her company, whether it be in hell or in heaven.

Savitri asked her husband, "My lord, what is it in me that makes you desire my company always?"

Mohan answered, "It is your beautiful face, sweet smile, affection, kindness, your curly hair, your rosy cheeks and scarlet lips. It is your gestures and your piercing glances, your melodious voice and songs that fascinate me."

Savitri then asked, "Suppose I lose my beauty and complexion on account of anaemia, or I get pits on my face on account of smallpox, or eruptions all over my body and my hair falls; suppose I treat you a little harshly or begin to love somebody else—would you still wish to remain in my company?"

Mohan was bewildered and stunned on hearing her words.

Savitri said, "Your love is only infatuation or passion for the body. It is not real love. It cannot last for ever. There is an immortal Self or Atman within the hearts of all beings. It is the fountain-source of all beauty. It is the Beauty of beauties. You have to realise this Atman through purification and meditation. Then only will your love last for ever. Give up this passion for my body. Turn your mind inward, dive deep into the recesses of your heart and behold the splendour of the Atman."

Mohan came to his senses. He prostrated before his wife and took her as his Guru. He plunged himself in spiritual Sadhana and attained Self-realisation.

53

RAGHAVAN AND HIS WIFE

RAGHAVAN WAS the son of a very wealthy Zamindar of Chidambaram in South India. He married Pankajam, the daughter of a landlord in Mayavaram.

Both Raghavan and his wife lived happily for some years. They had three sons and two daughters.

Once Raghavan speculated in business and lost some property. At this critical juncture, Pankajam asked her husband to have a necklace made, set with diamonds and rubies. Raghavan was unable to accede to her request, so she used to quarrel with him daily.

Raghavan finally became disgusted with his wife on account of this constant quarrelling and said to her one day, "Pankajam, as you are quarrelling with me daily, I will leave the house and take Sannyas in Benares."

Pankajam did not stop her quarrelling in spite of her husband's warning.

One day, Raghavan left the house and proceeded to Cuddalore. He stayed there for a week and then returned. He said to his wife, "Pankajam, I am now leaving the house forever. I will take Sannyas. But I want to tell you one thing: take great care of the house, property, cows and children."

Raghavan left the house and travelled directly to Benares. He approached Sri Swami Sankara Bharati and requested him, "Swamiji, kindly give me Sannyas. I will serve you with devotion. But Swamiji, you must give me coffee and salted *halwa* early in the morning and afternoon, and *sambar* and *rasam* also. I have renounced my wife, property and children but I have not yet renounced my coffee habit which I have had for the last forty-five years."

Sri Sankara Bharati was a pious and dispassionate Mahatma. He lived on alms. How could he supply our Raghavan with coffee, *halwa, sambar* and *rasam*?

The Swamiji said, "Raghavan, you would have to go back to your house. I live on alms here. I cannot give you all these things. You are not yet ready for Sannyas. Control the tongue. Practise Japa and austerities for some years and then come to me when you are able to live on dry bread alone."

Raghavan was in a great fix. He was unable to get on with the Swamiji. Furthermore, his mind was on his property, wife and children. So he immediately went back to Chidambaram.

Sannyas is made of more sterner stuff. Those who renounce the world on account of difficulties, who have not controlled their senses or disciplined their minds, who are not endowed with the four means of salvation, like peace, purity and other divine virtues, who have not removed the impurities and oscillations of the mind through selfless service and worship, will not be benefited by renouncing the world. They will have to share the fate of our friend Raghavan.

54

CONFERENCE OF MOSQUITOES AND BUGS

MOSQUITOES: "O LORD! Thou hast given us the proboscis to sting and suck blood. Thou hast created man with fresh and pure blood. Thou hast created us with tiny bodies and given us wings also to enable us to fly away when we are in danger. Thou hast given us the ability to pass on quickly from one man to another and drink blood to our heart's content. Thou art kind and merciful to our race. But why hast Thou created an enemy also? Mr. Wind is our only enemy. He is very cruel. We have not done him any harm but he drives us away and disturbs us when we enjoy our hearty meals. At the very appearance of Mr. Wind we have to go far, far away. What shall we poor creatures do? Have mercy and remove our enemy from this earth."

The Lord: "My children, you are all very dear to Me. I cannot decide the case without the presence of the accused. I shall send word to him. Let me hear his statement also. Then I shall decide the case and show justice."

The moment Mr. Wind approached the Durbar of the Lord, the mosquitoes had to flee for their lives. The Lord could not decide the case in the absence of any one of the parties. So He said, "O dear Mr. Wind! the mosquitoes have filed a serious complaint against you. When they come back we shall proceed with the case."

So long as Mr. Wind was with the Lord in His Durbar the mosquitoes could not approach.

Now a wise mosquito had an inspired suggestion: "Let us call for a round-table conference and find out means and methods of destroying our enemy."

Accordingly, invitations were sent to Messrs Bugs, Flies, Bees and other comrades. At the opening session of the conference, the mosquitoes addressed the bugs.

"Dear brothers, you are all very happy. You drink the blood of man to your heart's content. You live in his bed with him. You do not have any enemy at all. Our case is very pitiable indeed. Mr. Wind is our chief enemy. When he approaches we are driven away. We cannot approach man. Our endeavours are frustrated. Your lot is very enviable. Now we have assembled here to get suggestions for the destruction of our enemy."

Bugs: "Brothers, you have not understood the real nature of Maya. It is distance that lends enchantment to the view. A doctor thinks that the barrister is happier than himself. A businessman thinks that a professor in a college is happier as he enjoys many holidays. Even so, you think that we are happier. Our position is very miserable. Just listen to our story. We do not sting man like you. We do not injure him in any way. We know many devices and stratagems. We can suck his blood and yet he may not feel it. He may sleep soundly. We hide ourselves in the holes of the bed, underneath the pillows and in the corners of the carpets. When man begins to search for us, even when we are caught, we remain motionless and pretend to be dead. But man, in the mood of vengeance, crushes us ruthlessly in the end. There is no way of escape for us. We have no wings to fly. You fly away with the help of your wings. We think that you are very lucky. We want to approach the Lord and pray for wings or to create man without eyes. Then we will be perfectly content and happy. We will not have any more complaints."

Flies: "Brothers, we think that you are all happy. You drink the blood of man and move about in ecstasy. Our lot is very miserable indeed. Our suffering is indescribable. We sit on the body of man to suck his blood. He is very cruel. He drives us away immediately by giving us a good slap. We are not crushed as we escape in a mysterious manner. But we have to starve for many days. Though we are fond of blood, we cannot get even a drop. Let us all approach the Lord. We will pray to Him to create human beings without hands."

In the Durbar of His Divine Majesty, the bugs, mosquitoes and flies presented their grievances before the Lord. The Lord heard their statements patiently but kept quiet. He did not speak a word. Even God cannot decide such cases and cannot remove the grievances of all entirely.

In offices, Ashrams and institutions, those who have not evolved, fight amongst themselves out of jealousy, hatred and petty-mindedness and present all their grievances to their superiors. In such cases the superiors or heads will have to remain silent. Then only will there be peace.

Aspirants and clerks do not attempt to improve themselves by following the advice given by their masters or superiors. They have not understood the nature of Maya. They cling tenaciously to their egoistic habits and traits and allow their minds to move in the old ruts. What can the masters do when the students are arrogant, conceited, impertinent and self-assertive?

In this world, jealousy is the chief enemy of peace. It assumes the form of petty-mindedness and creates great havoc and mischief. It does not spare even educated people and Sannyasins either. It is the chief weapon of Maya.

When a Sannyasin becomes famous, others become jealous of him. It is easy to renounce wealth. It is easy to renounce wife and children; but it is extremely difficult to renounce name and fame.

He who has eradicated all forms of jealousy through the development of a magnanimous heart and Atma Bhav and enquiry of "Who am I?", is the happiest and most peaceful man in the world. People who are not content with their lot are restless and undergo suffering like the bugs, mosquitoes and flies. God has created every human being in this world with some conveniences and some inconveniences. Good and bad are both relative terms. Always see good in everything. Lead a simple and contented life and enjoy peace and bliss.

This is a relative world of pleasure and pain, good and bad, convenience and inconvenience, comfort and discomfort. You can find supreme peace in the Self only. Realise the Self and be free from all grievances, inconveniences and discomforts.

When there is one Self in all beings, how can one be jealous of another? How can one exploit another? How can one hate another? Behold the one Self in all beings and rest in the everlasting peace of the Eternal.

55

PRINCESS VIDYAVATI

PRINCESS VIDYAVATI became the ruler of the
Magadha Kingdom when she was only eighteen years
old. She was a very pious and cultured lady. She was
well versed in the study of the *Gita, Upanishads,
Brahma Sutras* and the six schools of philosophy. She
refused to get married although her parents and
relatives pressed her several times. She had discrimination and dispassion to a considerable degree. She
spent her time in meditation and study of the
Upanishads. She was an able ruler and politician also,
like Queen Chudalai.

Princess Vidyavati used to practise intense Tapas
and Sadhana and was a Self-realised soul. She
conducted classes in Vedanta daily in the afternoon
between 2 and 4p.m. Many Pundits and scholars used
to attend these classes. She cleared the doubts of all in
a wonderful manner.

A poor Brahmin priest also attended her classes
regularly. He used to come half an hour earlier and
leave the place after everyone had left. He used to take
his seat near the princess. People presumed that this
Brahmin priest was very interested in Vedanta.

One day, when the class was over, the Brahmin

priest followed the princess silently to her palace. The princess saw him only when she reached the palace. She gave him a cordial reception, offered him a seat and enquired, "Sir, how can I serve you?"

The Brahmin priest replied, "You are the most beautiful girl in the world. I am very much charmed by your beauty. I have an intense desire to marry you."

The princess replied, "I am delighted to know about your desire. I shall satisfy your wish."

The Brahmin was immensely pleased when his request was granted by the lady. He asked the princess, "Will you fix a date for our marriage?"

Princess: "Any day you choose."

Brahmin: "Tomorrow is the most auspicious day. May I come?"

Princess: "By all means."

Brahmin: "At what time should I come?"

Princess: "You can come at 2p.m."

Brahmin: "I am grateful to you. I am the most fortunate man in the world. I will come prepared for the nuptials. Kindly instruct the man at the gate to allow me to come inside with all my things. I shall bring all the things necessary for the nuptials.

In the presence of the Brahmin the princess called her men and gave orders to announce the marriage, and instructed the gatekeeper to permit him to come to her the following day at 2p.m. All her relatives and officers were stunned. They were grieved to hear that the princess was going to get married to a poor Brahmin priest.

The Brahmin left the palace and went directly to some money-lenders and borrowed a big amount at high interest. He purchased silk *saris*, a bed, pillows and other items. He spent a restless night.

172

Princess Vidyavati

The next day he dressed himself in silken clothes and turban and proceeded to the palace with all his things. The gatekeeper immediately allowed him into the palace. He entered the hall where Vidyavati was delivering her lecture on Vedanta. He bowed before her and took his seat with a majestic attitude. While the princess was discussing a very important point in Vedanta, he interrupted her and said, "I have brought all the necessary articles. May I fix up everything?"

The princess calmly replied, "O yes! you can. I will be ready presently."

In a short time the Brahmin priest decorated the cot and again interrrupted, saying, "It is getting late. Time is precious. You have fixed the nuptials for 2p.m. today. Have you forgotten this? Enough of your Vedanta. Keep to your promise."

Princess Vidyavati was an embodiment of patience. Nothing could disturb her peace of mind. She kept cool and balanced at all times and in all conditions, because she rested in her own essential divine nature. She replied, "Yes, I will attend to you first and then continue the class."

She stopped her lecture and took her seat on the cot which was arranged on the same platform. She said, "Dear sir, I am now ready for the nuptials. Come and take your seat by my side."

The Brahmin said, "You are an innocent girl. You do not know anything of worldly matters. This is a thing to be done privately and not in the presence of others. Therefore ask your servants to remove the cot to another room."

The princess said, "Never mind the public. Come and take your seat here. I cannot waste my time. Many are waiting for the class to continue. I must finish it."

173

The Brahmin became very nervous. He trembled before her. He spoke not a word. Then the princess got down from the cot and spoke to him, "You are a Brahmin. I am a *kshatriya* girl. You lost your senses under the influence of passion and are attempting for something that is beyond your reach. Is this a virtuous action for a Brahmin priest?

"You wish to do an evil action secretly. You need not be afraid of the public when you openly do a right action. The very idea that you want to do a thing secretly shows that you are attempting to do something which is not just and proper. Anything done in secret is a sin. Even if you do certain actions secretly, without the knowledge of the public, yet you cannot hide them from the Lord who is seated in your heart. He is watching all your actions. He knows your inner thoughts and motives. You cannot cheat Him, although you imagine that you can cheat the public. In cheating others you cheat yourself only. There is nothing but the Self. All indeed is the Self or Brahman. There is no diversity. This is the emphatic declaration of sages who have realised the Self. Never attempt to do evil actions. You will be ruined if you do.

"Another point is that the husband should be wiser and more powerful than the girl he chooses. He must be superior to her in every respect. Then only can he lead a peaceful family life. You tremble before me. You have no strength to stand before me. You sit at my feet when I offer you an equal seat. You speak to me in a low, begging voice. Are you a proper man for me to marry?

"You are over fifty. Many of your teeth have fallen. Your hair has become grey. Yet passion has not left you. You want to marry a young girl of another caste.

Being a Brahmin priest, you should possess dispassion, discrimination, tranquillity and control of the senses. You should practise meditation at this age. Is it proper on your part to behave in this manner?

"I find you are overpowered by passion. You have no power of discrimination. You have not realised the glory of a chaste life. You are running after the filthy, perishable body of a female to satisfy your senses and derive momentary pleasure. You have forgotten the fountain-head of beauty which is hidden in the chambers of your heart. You have not attempted to attain that immortal Essence which will give you eternal peace and everlasting bliss. You can attain the supreme seat by leading a life of virtue and treading the path of Truth. Though you have attended my classes for months, you have not gained anything. You have not done any spiritual practice. Kill this demon of lust by practising Brahmacharya and regular meditation. Know your true Self and be free. I shall lift you up from the quagmire of worldliness."

Now the Brahmin priest thought over the matter seriously. He came to his senses. He realised his folly and repented for his foolish action. He prostrated at the feet of Vidyavati, imploring her to initiate him into the mysteries of Kaivalya. He surrendered himself entirely to her and took her as his Guru. He followed her instructions implicitly and did intense penance. He disciplined his senses and developed divine qualities. Eventually he attained the goal of life—the final beatitude.

56

QUEEN KEKAYI

KEKAYI WAS THE queen of the king of Kekaya. She was the mother of Kaikeyi. The king of Kekaya possessed a sound knowledge of the language of beasts, birds and insects. This was conferred on him by sage Samika. The sage had conferred this boon and said, "O king! I give you this boon by which you will be able to know what the birds and beasts talk among themselves. But mind you, if you reveal any of their conversations to anyone to satisfy their curiosity, your head will burst into a thousand pieces."

One day, the king was seated with his queen in the garden. He observed an ant taking a grain of rice and hurrying with it to its hole. Meanwhile, another ant came across and said to it, "Friend, I am very hungry. Please give me that grain of rice."

The first ant replied, "No, I cannot, because you belong to a higher caste. You cannot accept the grain from me who am of a lower caste."

At this differentiation and petty distinction even amongst the little insignificant ants, the king burst into uncontrollable laughter.

The queen, who was sitting by his side, enquired of him the reason for his laughter. The king could not reveal the truth on account of the warning of the sage. He tried to evade the queen.

But the queen persisted. She said, "You are hiding something from me. I will not take meals or do anything until and unless you reveal this secret to me." The king was in a fix. He did not know what to do. At last he said, "My beloved, I am prohibited from telling you on account of the warning of Rishi Samika. If I tell you my head will burst into a thousand pieces. What am I to do now? Give up this obstinacy and save me."

The queen replied, "I do not mind what the consequences may be of your telling me. I do not care. I want to know the reason for the laughter."

Women of this type, like Kekayi and Kaikeyi, are many these days. They are obstinate and arrogant. This is unbecoming of them. They should be ideal wives like Nalayini and Savitri.

When the king found no means of appeasing the curiosity of his wife, he said to her after deep thought, "You want to know the secret even at the cost of my life. So then, I will reveal this to you at Benares, where dying, I shall attain liberation."

The next day the king and queen set out for Benares. Arriving there, the queen again pressed the king to reveal his secret. The king said, "I will tell you what it is after three days."

The king was sunk in sorrow, reflecting over his fate, and left for a lonely trip to the neighbouring hills. He went and sat underneath a tree. He was tired of walking and was very hungry also. Suddenly he overheard a quarrel between two goats. The she-goat was saying to the he-goat, "Get me the grass hanging in the well otherwise I will not live with you. I will part with you forever."

The he-goat replied, "What a fool you are! Do you not see that it is risky to get to the grass over there? I will fall into the waterless pit and die."

The she-goat said, "I do not care about that. I want that grass only."

The he-goat got furious and butted the she-goat with his horns so severely that she began to bleed profusely. The she-goat gave up her obstinacy and begged for pardon.

The king got the clue. He went back to his palace. The queen as usual insisted on his revealing his secret. The king then took a long cane and thrashed her severely right and left, saying, "I will kill you today if you persist in this query. What do you want now? Tell me frankly, do you still insist on hearing the secret?"

The queen was terrified at this behaviour of the king. She begged his pardon and said, "No, my lord. Save me. I do not want to know any of your secrets. Pray, stop this cruel treatment. Let us live happily from today."

The mind is also persistent like the queen of Kekaya. O aspirants! be on the alert. Do not yield to temptations. Your boat will capsize if you are careless. Do not allow the water to enter the boat. Sail smoothly on the waters. Live in the world but do not let the taint of the world affect you. Conquer Maya. Use the iron rod of discrimination, cut the knot of ignorance and soar high in the realms of peace and bliss.

May you all overcome lust, anger and greed! May you become Jivanmuktas in this very life!

57

LOOK TO THE BHAV

THERE LIVED a king named Raja Singh Bahadur in Bihar. There was a big Ashram for Sannyasins in Anandapuri.

Once the Diwans and ministers reported to the king that the Sannyasins and Brahmacharis at the Ashram were always engaged in eating sweetmeats and *kheer*. They spent most of their time in sleeping and were not doing any austerities, spiritual practices or meditation. There was a feast at the Ashram at least once a week.

The king sent a messenger to bring the Mahant, Swami Niralambananda, to his presence. The Mahant came to see the king.

"The Diwans and ministers have reported to me," said the king, "that the Swamis and Brahmacharis are not doing any Sadhana. They are only eating sweetmeats and sleeping."

"Please," replied Niralambananda, "come to the Ashram in the early morning and you will know the true facts. I will come and wake you up at three in the morning."

The next morning Swami Niralambananda went to the palace and woke the king at three o'clock. He asked the king's attendant to take along with them a pot of water. They went first to the homes of the Diwans and ministers.

The Swami asked the attendant to throw water on the faces of the sleeping Diwans and ministers. They all woke up uttering, "bloody fool", "ass", "damn nonsense", "who has disturbed my sleep?"

The king and the Swami then went to the stable. The Swami asked the attendant to throw water on the faces of the grooms. They also woke up uttering, "sala", "badmash", etc.

Thereupon the party proceeded to the Ashram. Water was then thrown on the faces of the Sannyasins and Brahmacharis. They all awoke uttering "Sivoham", "Hari Om", "Ram, Ram".

"Look here, O king!" said the Swami, "have you noted the difference now? Have you noted the attitude, feeling and the words that came out of the mouths of these different kinds of people? The words reveal the contents of the heart and mind and show the culture of the persons.

"Sadhus and Sannyasins also work and take food, but the attitude is different. Worldly people judge persons by their external actions. Sannyasins take food for the maintenance of the body. They have no idea of agency. They do not fill their stomachs to please the palate, to fatten themselves and utilise the energy in sensual indulgence. They work as witnesses of their actions. They work for the good of the world. They know that hunger is a characteristic of the physical sheath and not of the Self or Atman. They do not identify themselves with the body, mind, Prana, senses and intellect. They have the all-pervading Atma-Bhav. They may eat sweetmeats today, fast fully

tomorrow and take a few groundnuts only the following day. They may dress themselves in silk today and
in rags and gunny bags tomorrow. They may sleep on
fine beds with cushions today; tomorrow they may
even sleep on the bare stone floor. Their ways are
mysterious. Worldly people cannot understand them,
for they are Maha-Kartas, Maha-Tyagis and Maha-
Bhogis."

The Swami went on to add, "They have no thought
of the world. Their motives are always pure. Their
thoughts are pure. They have no thought of the
morrow. They always fill their minds with pure, sublime thoughts. They never think: 'What will I get by
doing this action? How much money will I make from
this?' These thoughts never occupy their minds. Their
only thoughts will be: 'How can I serve the world to the
maximum degree? How can I make the people ethical
and religious-minded? How can I make them Yogis
and Jnanis? How can I make them happy and wise?'

"They may appear to you to be sitting silent, as if
Tamasic, but internally they are vibrant, radiant, full of
purity and elevating thoughts.

"O king! judge not people by external acts. Look to
their motives and attitude.

"A Sannyasin," went on the Swami, "will not keep
anything for himself. He will always share what he has
with others. Whenever there is any calamity in the
land, he will dedicate his life in doing such deeds as
will relieve human suffering. He lives to serve. When
the test comes to sacrifice life, you will discover the
difference between a householder and a Sannyasin.

"They do not care for feasts," the Swami laughed.
"They always want simple food—*dhal* and bread. To
bring auspiciousness and prosperity to the people,

181

they arrange feasts at their sincere request."

"O adorable Swamiji!" said the king, "please pardon me. Now I understand the philosophy of motives and internal attitudes. Your remarks have been illuminating, inspiring and instructive. They have opened my eyes. I was judging people only by their external actions. You have imparted inspiring knowledge to me. I shall be ever grateful to you, O revered Swamiji! Crores of prostrations and adorations unto thee! Om Namo Narayanaya! Thou art my Guru from now on!"

The king sings:

Guru Maharaj Guru Maharaj Guru Maharaj
Pahimaam,
Para Brahman Sadguru Maharaj Rakshamaam.

58

KING SAKUNTA

SRI VASISHTHA once performed a certain Yajna which was attended by many sages, Rishis, Munis and kings. Narada, Viswamitra and Sakunta, the king of Kasi, were also present.

At the time of departure, Sakunta made prostrations to sage Vasishtha first and then to the others.

After some months Narada Rishi paid a visit to Rishi Viswamitra and said to him in the course of his talk, "O adorable Rishi! your prestige as a prominent Rishi is gradually vanishing now."

"Why is it so, my beloved Narada?"

The sage replied, "Don't you remember, O Rishi! that King Sakunta paid respects to sage Vasishtha first and then to you and the rest. Since then I hear only the name of Vasishtha wherever I go. There would have been no harm if Sakunta saluted you first and then Vasishtha. As you did not punish Sakunta for the disrespect, others are also following his example."

Viswamitra said, "O Narada! is it due solely to that incident that I am lowered in the estimation of others? If it is so I must punish Sakunta or I must attain eminence by doing severe penance. What do you advise now, O great Rishi?"

183

"Adorable Rishi Viswamitraji! the behaviour of the king on that occasion was not good. This has lowered your rank in the estimation of others. Really you are a great Tapasvin. You are not in any way inferior to Vasishtha."

Viswamitra in a rage said, "Sakunta has ruined my fame. Why should I not ruin him now? Why should I not curse him?"

Narada said, "That is indeed a proper punishment, but you must not lose your power of austerity by taking recourse to that method. I will suggest a suitable plan. You may adopt it if you approve of it. Kindly ask your courageous disciple, Sri Rama, to punish Sakunta."

Viswamitra at once proceeded to Ayodhya and met Sri Rama. He said to Rama, "O Rama! are you not bound to keep up my prestige and reputation?"

Rama replied, "My adorable Guru, I am certainly bound to keep up thy honour and reputation."

"Then, by sunset tomorrow, kill that man who has lowered my reputation," said Viswamitra.

"My worthy Guru, I shall carry out thy behest. I shall act accordingly. May I know the name of the person?"

"Sakunta, the king of Kasi."

Viswamitra then returned to his Ashram.

Narada proceeded to Sakunta and said, "O king! you are a great devotee of Lord Rama. Despite your devotion to Him, He is going to kill you before sunset tomorrow."

"O adorable Rishi Narada! Lord Rama can kill me and my whole family. We are quite ready to die at His hands. But we do not wish to die as His enemies. This gives me great anguish."

Narada then said, "O King Sakunta! do not be disheartened. Be bold. Be courageous. Use your intelligence and try to secure help from others."

"No one will help me. I do not wish to bring trouble to others. I am prepared to die. I shall myself appear before Lord Rama prior to the appointed time."

"Never despair. Some wise and powerful man may protect you without violating the vows of Rama. Please try," advised Narada.

"O wise Rishi! please tell me how I can get the help of such a person."

"O King! go to the forest and speak out loudly: 'Is there anyone who can save me from danger? Let him appear before me and protect me.' If anyone comes before you tell him all about your trouble."

The king placed his son on the throne immediately and went into the forest. He called out for help. Anjanidevi, mother of Sri Hanuman, heard the shout and immediately appeared from her cave.

She said, "O man! what is your trouble? Why are you weeping? I will save you from your danger. Let me know all about it in detail."

Sakunta said, "O venerable lady! give me assurance then I will tell you everything in detail."

"Do not doubt me. I promise in the name of my dear son that I will protect you from danger. Please tell me all about it."

Sakunta said, "Lord Rama has determined to kill me today before sunset. Save me from this danger."

"What a terrible mistake I have committed on account of my pride of strength and egoism! I should not have given my promise before having the knowledge of the service to be rendered. My son is most devoted to Rama. Had it not been for the promise I myself might have killed this man and done some real service to Lord Rama. I cannot break my promise. There is conflict of duty in my mind now."

Anjanidevi hid in a cave and shouted, "O most beloved son! come to me at once."

Hanuman immediately appeared before her and said, "O beloved mother! what is the matter? Is there any service required of me?"

"My dear Hanuman, I am in great trouble. Save me. I have given word of promise to Sakunta to save him from danger. Now I cannot break my promise. Please save him from the arrows of Lord Rama."

Hanuman decided to conceal Sakunta within the ample coils of his tail, sit on the top of a hill and meditate on Lord Rama and chant His Name.

Lord Rama sent Satrughna to bring Sakunta before Him. Satrughna proceeded to Benares, but did not find Sakunta there. He got news that the king had gone to a neighbouring forest. He went to the forest and continued his search. He saw Hanuman sitting on top of a hill. He approached him and enquired of Sakunta.

Hanuman said, "O Satrughna! I am keeping Sakunta within my coiled up tail in order to uphold the words of my mother. Kill me first and then take him away to your brother."

Satrughna said, "O adorable Hanuman! you are the greatest devotee of Lord Rama. You have extraordinary powers. You once saved me from death. I regard you as my own brother. You are blessed as a Chiranjeevi by Sri Sita. I am not prepared to kill you. Even if I attempt it, I will certainly fail in my attempt."

Satrughna returned to his place and informed Lord Rama that he had no strength to bring Sakunta.

At once Lakshmana started out in order to bring Sakunta. Satrughna secretly told Lakshmana the real

story. Lakshmana departed but returned without the
king. Then Bharata went to bring Sakunta, but he also
returned and plainly narrated the facts to Lord Rama.
Thereupon Lord Rama Himself proceeded to the
spot where Hanuman was. All the brothers accompanied Him. Lord Rama saw Hanuman, who prostrated to his Lord and again sat in meditation.

Lord Rama said, "O beloved Hanuman! I must kill
Sakunta in order to carry out the behests of my Guru.
Surrender him to me."

Hanuman said, "O Lord! I am forced to save Sakunta
to keep the words of my mother. Please kill me and
then kill Sakunta."

"O Hanuman! get ready for the fight."

Lord Rama then discharged an arrow at Hanuman.
It fell like a beautiful garland around the neck of
Hanuman. Rama sent many arrows but they all had no
effect. In the end He sent the powerful Narayana Astra.
This produced terrible heat everywhere. All the Devas
ran here and there for safety and at last fell at the feet
of Brahma.

Hanuman was all along repeating the Rama Mantra:
"Sri Ram Jaya Ram Jaya Jaya Ram". Brahma appeared
on the spot with the Devas. He asked Hanuman to
open his eyes. Hanuman opened them and found
Brahma and others before him. At once Hanuman fell
at the feet of Brahma. Brahma asked him to prostrate at
the feet of Rishi Viswamitra who was also there.
Hanuman did so and received the blessings of the
Rishi. When Hanuman got up, Viswamitra found that
King Sakunta also had been prostrating at his feet.

Viswamitra then said loudly, "O dear Rama! please
do not kill Sakunta because he has fallen at my feet. I
must save him now, otherwise I shall incur sin."

Lord Rama obeyed the words of Rishi Viswamitra. Thus the fight ended. Sri Hanuman fell at the feet of Lord Rama and begged to be forgiven.

Lord Rama said, "O my beloved devotee! I am immensely pleased with you. You are the foremost among My devotees. You have shown to the world the power of the Rama-Mantra."

Lord Rama embraced Hanuman and blessed him.

Narada also appeared on the scene and prostrated at the feet of Lord Rama and said, "Please pardon me for the mischief and trouble I have created."

Lord Rama said, "O Rishi! you always do immense good to the world by creating some kind of quarrel. You have pleased Me very much by creating this trouble."

To the king, Lord Rama said, "O. Sakunta! through you only the glory of the Rama-Mantra has been made known to the world. Great devotees and sages ever select virtuous persons like you for proving true principles to the world. Return to your kingdom and be happy. I am greatly pleased with you."

Now Anjanidevi came before Lord Rama and said, "Please pardon me and my son for our wrong actions."

Lord Rama said, "Even the mistake of a true devotee towards his Beloved brings great good to the devotees and others. I am pleased with you too."

Lord Rama blessed all those who were present. All went back to their respective places in great joy.

The glory of Ram-Nam is indescribable. Ram-Nam is your sole refuge or prop in this world to cross the formidable ocean of Samsara and attain immortality and eternal bliss.

Glory to Lord Rama and Sri Hanuman! Glory to Ram-Nam!

59

SULOCHANA

GUPTA BABU was a Tahsildar. He lived in Calcutta. His son, Narendra, was a graduate of the Calcutta University. He was a very fashionable boy. He was an up-to-date gentleman. His father wanted Narendra to marry Sushila, the daughter of a poor man. She was a very pious girl who knew Sanskrit and had studied the *Gita, Upanishads, Ramayana* and *Bhagawata*. She could sit in Padmasana for three hours at a stretch for Japa and meditation. She could sing beautifully the songs of Tulsidas and Surdas.

But Narendra did not want to marry Sushila. He wanted to marry Sulochana, a very fashionable girl, who had studied many modern novels and who was also a graduate of the Calcutta University. The lives of Mirabai, Savitri, Madalasa and Gargi did not appeal to Sulochana. She used to draw inspiration from the stars of the silver screen. She had learnt the art of hoodwinking the hubby. She could play the piano also.

Narendra eventually married Sulochana. They both lived happily. They used to walk along the beach with clasped hands. Sulochana would appear in her new, loose, fashionable, semi-transparent blouse or gown in front of Narendra. They both used to walk along the Chowringhee Road for shopping. Sulochana would put her hand around the neck of Narendra while walking along the road. Narendra enjoyed her company very much.

One day Narendra had to go to his office at 8 o'clock in the morning. He said to Sulochana, "My dear, I have to go to the office a little earlier than usual. My officer is coming today for inspection. Kindly prepare the breakfast now."

Sulochana was reading the newspaper as there was some sensational news and an interesting editorial column in it.

She said, "Please wait for ten minutes. Let me finish the editorial column first."

Narendra came after ten minutes and said, "Dear Sulochana, it is getting late. Please prepare the tea immediately."

Sulochana did not get up. She was reading the newspaper with great interest and attention. Again Narendra came after fifteen minutes and said in an angry tone, "Sulochana, what are you doing? What is the matter with you today? Did you not hear me? Get up and prepare the tea at once. I am in a hurry."

Sulochana was offended. She retorted, "Look here! Don't talk so much. You are a graduate. I am also a graduate. Why should I serve you? Why don't you prepare the tea yourself and serve me?"

Narendra was put to great shame. He hung his head and quietly left the place. He himself prepared the tea and went to the office. In the evening he went to a solitary place in a garden and thought within himself: "What a great fool I was? I was carried away by this fashionable girl. My wise father wanted me to marry

190

Sushila. Sushila, though poor, is a pious, devoted girl. I would have been very happy had I married her. She would have been very obedient to me. Look at the arrogant nature of this fashionable and wretched girl, Sulochana. How contemptuously she treated me. I cannot live with her even for a single second."

Such is the condition of fashionable men and women who have no purity, devotion and ethical training. It is very difficult for a poor man to get on with an expensive, ease-loving fashionable girl. It is better for a man to marry a poor girl who is devoted and has divine virtues. It is better for a girl also to marry a poor but devoted man than one who is proud and fashionable.

60

THE STORY OF KALI

KALI APPEARED before Rajah Parikshit. The Rajah said to him, "O Kali! there is no place for you in my dominion. You must leave my territory immediately."

Kali was very much grieved on hearing the words of the Rajah. He said, "O Rajah! do not be so cruel to me. Thou art an embodiment of mercy and righteousness. Be merciful to me. Where can I go? Give me some sort of shelter in your dominion."

Rajah Parikshit then gave four places to Kali—the gambling house; the slaughtering place where animals are killed; the place where sisters of ill-fame live; the place where people drink intoxicating liquor.

Kali then said to the Rajah, "O Rajah! it will be difficult for me to reside in so many places at the same time. Be pleased to give me one place where all these will be found together."

The Rajah pondered for three or four days and then said, "I have found out a very suitable place for you. You will now be greatly pleased to occupy that place."

The Rajah presented a ball of gold to Kali and said, "Take your abode in money; you will find all the above four and one more element, enmity."

Kali said, "Well said, O merciful Rajah! I am really

very happy now. I can now work wonders with money. How kind you are! I will bring thousands of people into my clutches. I will make them quite restless. I will create quarrels among them. I will delude the worldly-minded people. I will make them drink liquor. I will induce them to spend all their money in gambling, and thus make them beggars. I will make them meat-eaters and increase their animal passion."

Wealth is evil. Wealth is at the root of all evil. It produces intoxication in the mind. It generates pride. It makes a man forget God. Rich people are stone-hearted. Lord Jesus says: "It is easier for a camel to enter the eye of a needle than for a rich man to enter the Kingdom of Heaven."

Wealth can never be accumulated without injuring others. It begets various vices. The poor man who worships God, though he is clad in rags, though he has nothing to eat, is the wealthiest man in the whole world. He is very dear to the Lord. Spiritual wealth is the real wealth. It is eternal. It cannot be plundered by dacoits. Therefore obtain this imperishable spiritual wealth and move about happily. Now Kali will not dare touch you. Lord Yama, the God of Death, will not dare entrap you.

61

STORY OF GANDHARI

IN THE GREAT Mahabharata war between the Pandavas and the Kauravas, all the Kauravas were killed. The Kauravas were the sons of Gandhari. Gandhari was overcome with great sorrow. She took the dead body of Duryodhana on her lap and wailed aloud. She sat in the same spot till sunset. Everyone had returned to their own places except Gandhari, who did not like to part with her dead sons. Great was her attachment to her children.

Lord Krishna appeared on the spot and said to her, "O Mother! enough of this vain sorrow. Why do you weep over the inevitable separation from your sons? Sons and relations are all united for selfish ends. They pass away from this world just as travellers depart from each other in front of a public inn. You are wailing over that for which you should not feel sorry. They will never come back to life. What is death? It is a mere change of the outer cloak. The inner Atman never dies nor is it ever born. Come, let us go home. You cannot bear hunger. Hunger is the harasser of all beings. It is getting dark now."

Gandhari said, "O Krishna! You are the cause of this calamity. Do not persuade me to go back home. I shall

194

never go back. I shall die with my children. Nothing interests me any more after the death of my children. I shall fast unto death. I shall not eat anything."

When Krishna found that Gandhari was adamant, He left the place quietly.

Two days passed. Gandhari could not get anything to eat. She felt very hungry. She searched all round. At last she found a piece of dog's flesh hanging from the branch of a nearby tree. She looked around and found no one present. She decided to eat the dog's flesh just to appease her hunger. But the tree was tall. She could not reach it from the ground. So she piled the dead bodies of her own sons on top of one another and climbed up, She caught hold of the dog's flesh and was about to put it into her mouth when Krishna, the Indweller of all hearts, made His appearance and said, "O Mother! refrain from eating dog's flesh. I have brought delicious food for you. Take it to your heart's content. When I am here to serve you, why should you suffer like this? I told you that hunger is a great harasser of living beings. No one can conquer it."

Gandhari hung her head in shame and remorse. She fell at the feet of Krishna and said, "O Krishna! Thou art the Antaryamin, the Indweller of all beings. Thou art the Lord of this world. Please remove my ignorance and lead me on to light and knowledge. Let me give up this attachment to my children, which is hard to give up."

Krishna and Gandhari then arrived at the palace of Yudhisthira where the noble Dharmaputra honoured them.

Great is the torture of hunger. Great is the torture of attachment. Friends, greater still is the bond of Karma. Greatest of all is this clinging to the body. Kill this body-idea. Destroy egoism. Remove ignorance and eradicate selfishness. Give up attachment to wife and children, wealth and home. Become perfectly dispassionate and detached. This is the key to unlock the domain of Elysian bliss, joy and immortality.

62

FORBEARANCE—THE TEST OF SAINTLINESS

A SPIRITUAL ASPIRANT once went to a certain saint and said, "Sir, tell me the means by which I may obtain a vision of God."

The saint advised him to retire into seclusion and apply himself to uninterrupted prayer for one full year.

"On the completion of the year," the saint further advised, "after having thoroughly subdued and annihilated your egoism, come to me after taking a bath."

According to this advice of the saint the aspirant started prayer in right earnest.

A sweeper used to come to sweep the ground around the hut of the saint. On the day when the aspirant was to complete his one year of Sadhana, the saint called the sweeper aside and, mentioning the place where the aspirant was living, said, "There is a person engaged in worship of God at that place. When he finishes his bath this morning, scatter dust over him with your broom."

The sweeper did as he was instructed. This upset the aspirant very much. In a fit of anger he ran after the sweeper to beat him.

"The scoundrel has thoroughly defiled me," he said,

and, taking bath for the second time, came to the hermitage of the saint.

"Sir, one full year has been completed since you gave me your instructions. May I now have the privilege of having the vision of the Lord?"

The saint replied, "Child, your mind is not yet subdued. Even now you run in anger to bite like a venomous snake. Go and worship for one year more and destroy the mind."

The aspirant therefore retired again and engaged himself in prayer for another year.

On the day when the second year was to be completed, the saint instructed the sweeper to touch the aspirant with his broom when the latter finished his bath. The sweeper did exactly as he was told. This time the aspirant did not run after the sweeper to beat him, but rebuked him with harsh and unbecoming words. Then, taking bath again, he went to the saint with his prayer for the vision of God.

The saint said, "The serpent of your mind even now emits terrible and fearful hisses. How can you expect to see God without killing it? Go and apply yourself to your practice of prayer for another year. But take care, if you fail in the test the next time, God will not favour you with His vision."

This time the aspirant carried on his spiritual practices with great determination. On the day when he was to complete the third year of practice, the saint asked the sweeper to throw upon him the entire lot of dirt that he had collected that morning. The sweeper carried out this instruction also, but the aspirant had now conquered anger. Bowing before the sweeper, he said with unaffected humility, "Brother, you have done me a great favour. Had you not done this, how could I have freed myself from the grip of anger? I thank you from the bottom of my heart."

Then, once more the aspirant approached the saint. The saint blessed and initiated him. The aspirant did rigorous spiritual practice according to the advice of the teacher and soon had the vision of the Lord.

63

SAINT MALIDAS

IN THE PROVINCE of Bihar there was a cowherd boy
named Malidas. He was quite illiterate, but innocent
and pure. He used to graze his cows in the jungle
throughout the day and return home in the evening.

One day a Brahmin came there, took his bath in the
river and sat on the bank, doing Pranayama and
worship of the Lord. The boy keenly watched the
Brahmin. When the latter had finished his worship
and was departing, the boy at once caught hold of his
feet and requested him to tell him what he had been
doing. The Brahmin said that he had been doing Puja
(worship) of the Lord. Then the boy requested the
Brahmin to explain what Puja was.

Brahmin: "Puja is worship of the Lord by repeating
the Gayatri Mantra."

Malidas: "What is worship and Gayatri?"

Brahmin: "You are an illiterate boy. You cannot
understand all these things. Please let me go."

Malidas: "All right, you may go. But tell me one
thing."

Brahmin: "What is it you wish to know?"

Malidas: "Why did you close your nose while doing
Puja?"

Brahmin: "By closing the nose, the breath is stopped and the mind gets concentrated. Through due concentration we see God."

Malidas: "Very well, now you may go."

The Brahmin went away. The boy Malidas accepted him as his Guru. He took bath in the river and sat down, closing his nose with his fingers. After a minute he began to think: "God has not yet come. Perhaps He will come late. So let me continue it." He was firm in his faith and yearned strongly: "I must see God."

After another minute had passed he became restless but did not open his nose.

Lord Vishnu was moved by the firm faith, innocent nature and purity of heart of the boy. The Lord saw that if He failed to appear before him, he would suffocate. So He revealed Himself. The boy saw before him a peculiar form with four hands and discs, and asked Him who He was.

The Lord: "I am God. I have come to give you Darshan as you closed your nose."

The boy: "How can I believe that you are God?"

Lord: "I am telling you the truth. You may satisfy yourself any way you like."

Boy: "I will call my Guru, and if he says so, then I will be satisfied."

Lord: "Very well, go and call him."

Boy: "But you may go away by that time."

Lord: "No, I will not go. I will remain here till you come back."

Boy: "But how can I believe you?"

Lord: "Then do as you like."

Boy: "I will tie you to this tree with a rope."

Lord: "Very well, please yourself."

The boy took a rope from a cow's neck and tied the

201

Lord to a tree and at once ran to fetch his Brahmin Guru. He found and caught hold of the Brahmin.

The Brahmin asked, "What is the matter? Why do you catch hold of me?"

The boy replied, "Guruji, please come quickly with me and see whether He is God or not."

The Brahmin thought that the boy was a fool. But the boy did not allow him to proceed further. At last the Brahmin went to the spot but he did not see anything. The boy pointed out to him the Lord who was tied with a rope to the tree. The Brahmin was not pure at heart and so he could not see the Lord. He was very much annoyed and had no patience. So, to get rid of the boy, he said, "Yes, this is the Lord."

The boy let the Brahmin go after doing the usual *namaskar*, and untied Lord Vishnu. Lord Vishnu was very pleased with him for his faith in the words of his Guru and requested him to ask any boon according to his liking.

The boy said, "I want nothing. I have sufficient food to maintain my body." The Lord again and again urged him to ask for something.

Finally the boy asked Him, "If you are pleased with me, then kindly give me this boon—as soon as I close my nose you should at once come to me. You should not delay as before."

Lord Vishnu was greatly pleased with his simplicity and said, "Your desire shall be fulfilled."

Now the boy found a playmate everyday. He would let the cows graze in the jungle and then close his nose. Lord Vishnu would come and play with him throughout the day.

After many years the same Brahmin happened to come that way. The boy fell at his feet and said,

"Guruji, you have shown me a very good method of seeing God."

The Brahmin could not understand him. Then the boy narrated the whole story from the very beginning. The Brahmin asked the boy to show him the Lord. The boy closed his nose and the Lord appeared. The boy requested his Guru to see the Lord but the Brahmin could not see Him as he was proud of his knowledge and not pure at heart.

The boy then requested the Lord to give Darshan to his Guru. The Lord said, "He is not pure. Let him purify his heart first and let him also give up his pride. Then only can he see Me."

Hearing this, the Brahmin abandoned his pride. He wept bitterly and fell at the feet of the boy. Then Lord Vishnu gave the Brahmin also His Darshan. Thus, through firm faith the boy saw the Lord and also showed Him to his Guru. Although at first the Guru deceived the boy, he had intense and firm faith in his Guru and in his words. Therefore have faith. Faith can do anything.

64

KEEP THY WORD

YOU SHOULD always keep your word. Failure in this respect brings in its wake a multitude of mishaps. You make enemies of friends. In spiritual life you take so many resolves but you do not stick to them. You take a vow to do this and not to do that. But the intensity of faith weakens and slowly you swerve from the right path. Progress on the spiritual path, as also success in worldly life, is impossible if you do not cultivate this cardinal virtue of keeping your resolves.

Sometimes we play this trick with the gods also. When we are afflicted, when we suffer from some disease, when we are forced to look to the gods for help, we promise to do some charity, to offer some special prayers. When we tide over the critical period, when we are well again, we forget all about it. God is omnipresent and omnipotent. He is omniscient. He knows our thoughts. How foolish it is to try to deceive Him!

Once a villager's son fell sick. One day the fever took a sudden turn for the worse. It was diagnosed as typhoid. No medicine could cure him.

The villager prayed to Mother Durga: "O Mother! please cure my boy's fever. O Durga! please save us from this peril. As soon as he gets well I shall take him to your shrine and offer special worship and *prasad* worth Rs. 100."

Through the Grace of Mother Durga the boy quickly got well. The old man remembered his promise to the Mother but thought: "I have already spent a good amount on medicine and doctor's fees. The doctor has also advised the boy to take a tonic to tone up his system. I am very hard up. I shall offer only Rs. 50 worth of *prasad* to Durga. She knows my position and will understand."

Days and weeks passed. Slowly he began to console himself with the idea: "After all, Durga is not going to eat Rs. 50 worth of sweets. Do not the scriptures say that God is more easily pleased with the attitude than with the physical offering of worship. I am a poor man. She knows it. So why waste so much money on sweets. Instead, I shall do a special worship and shall offer sweets for Rs. 5 only."

Even this remained only in the realm of thought for quite some time.

The house of the villager was very near the Durga temple. One day, while sitting alone in his room, he heard the temple bell ringing. This suddenly brought to his mind the promise he had given to the Mother. He was afraid of incurring the wrath of Durga. So he got up and went out immediately with Rs. 5.

On the way a friend enquired of his mission and, on being told, said, "Don't be silly. Is Mother Durga going to eat Rs. 5 worth of sweets? It is only foolishness that makes you think that way. What would surely satisfy Her is sincere worship at Her altar; and that you can do by merely purchasing some worship materials and a few coconuts for Rs. 1 and offering them to Her with sincere devotion. You can distribute these coconuts to the children inside the temple itself."

The old man was convinced of the fairness of this advice. He went to a shop nearby and enquired about the price of a coconut. He was told that it cost five annas each. He bargained and wanted four coconuts at the rate of four annas each. The shopkeeper, however, would not agree, but said, "If you want to buy it at four annas you will get it in the coconut garden which is a mile away from here."

The old man went to the place and saw a few coconut shops there. He was offered the coconuts at four annas each. He thought this price too high after having walked such a long distance. He wanted them at two annas each. The shopkeeper laughed and said, "You can't get them for that price here. You must go further to the grove itself."

The old miser pursued his quest. In the grove he enquired of the man in charge and was told that the price per coconut was two annas.

"What!" he thought, "I have come all this way to the grove itself. This man has just taken them out from the tree and wants two annas each for them."

He bargained here also and was told, "If you want it for one anna, you will have to take it yourself from the tree."

The power of greed is indescribable. The old man climbed up a tree. Not being trained in the art of climbing, he lost his hold while tugging at a coconut and jerked off his perch. He dangled high up, clinging to the coconut.

While he was in this precarious condition, the spirit of the Goddess possessed the body of the gardener who was Her worshipper and who had been praying for Rs. 100 for the marriage of his daughter. Mother Durga made the gardener demand Rs. 100 from the poor man hanging from the tree. The man, seeing no alternative, promised the amount. The gardener then managed to get him down.

The gardener went with him to his house and got his Rs. 100, which the old man gave with not a little hesitation. That night he reflected deeply over the incident and it suddenly dawned on him that the trouble was due to his not keeping his promise in the first place. He not only had to undergo all the suffering but could not escape the fulfilment of his original promise either.

Early the next morning he went to the temple and prayed to Mother Durga with tears in his eyes for pardon, promising at the same time that he would not repeat the same mistake.

This story has a twofold lesson for us. God knows our innermost thoughts and bestows His blessings on us or punishes us according to the good or bad thoughts we entertain. Secondly, keeping our word is of the utmost importance. If we realise how essential a quality it is for ordinary day-to-day living, we will readily see how very great the necessity is of strictly adhering to this virtue on the spiritual path. We often take resolves at holy places, but they are soon forgotten when we get back to our old surroundings. This is dangerous. No one can hope to have an iota of progress on the spiritual path if he does not sincerely stick to his promise. The motto should be: make few promises but stick to them tenaciously.

65

THE NATURE OF SAMSAR

ONCE UPON A time a certain king, while out hunting, was chased by an enraged tiger and her three cubs. Fleeing in great fear for his very life, the king suddenly fell into an old, deep and dark well. As he fell headlong, he managed somehow to catch hold of a plant that was growing on the side of the well about half way down. Clinging tightly to the plant, the unfortunate man remained suspended thus in the semi-darkness while the ferocious tiger sat growling above, seeking some means of springing upon him.

The little plant, unable to bear the weight, began to crack. Down in the waters of the well a crocodile waited with open jaws to snap at the king when he fell. A snake, long and venomous, also crawled along the plant towards the king to deliver its deadly bite. At this moment, two rats began to gnaw with their sharp teeth at the roots of the plant that was already on the point of snapping under the strain.

At this juncture there fell a drop of honey from a beehive built on the branch of a tree above the well. A breed of deadly insects had injected their venom into the hive and had rendered this honey into veritable poison.

The Nature of Samsar

In this pitiable and precarious condition, with a terrible and imminent death upon him, the doomed king put out his tongue to taste the drop of honey. This is what worldly life is like. Man suffers under the strain of cares, worries, pains and sufferings. In this precarious condition he still attempts to enjoy sensual pleasures, which are indeed poison.

The tree can be compared to the earthly domain; the tiger and the three cubs to lust, anger, greed and infatuation; the two rats to the day and night that cut short man's life; the snake and the crocodile to death above and below. In this miserable condition the man of the world tries to taste pleasure, even as the king tried to taste the honey. This earthly sensual pleasure is a veritable venom destructive of the soul of man.

Under the circumstances the only way left for the king was to have submitted himself to the protection of the Supreme Being. Similarly, man should, in spite of the numerous temptations and difficulties on earth, strive to attain God-realisation.

66

A BEGGAR MADE A MILLIONAIRE

THE DISCUSSION on the front verandah of Krishna Sastri's little house was lively and loud. Sankaran, a youthful neighbour and a recent *B.Com*,. was maintaining heatedly that it was absurd to say that God can do anything whatsoever and that there was no limit to His omnipotence. Krishna Sastri, on the contrary, was attempting to convince him that there was nothing impossible for Him.

A fair and handsome man, clad in the ochre robes of a Sannyasin and with a strange light of calmness and serenity radiating from his countenance, was passing down the roadway. He heard the loud discussion in progress. He paused in his stride and approached the debating assembly. The moment he drew near a hush fell upon the debaters and all eyes turned towards the strange Sadhu.

"I could not help," said the Sadhu, "hearing your remarks a little while ago. Never for a moment doubt God's omnipotence. He can do anything that He chooses to do. There is nothing impossible for Him. Listen, I shall illustrate this truth by relating a true incident.

"In the little Kabadawala quarter of the flourishing

city of Tirujpur, is a small, unostentatious yet neat looking temple of Lord Ganesha. Years ago a saint and mystic lived in the temple structure and used to worship the idol of Ganesha daily. The Deity was reputed as being of great power and truth and believed to grant the prayers of sincere devotees. Near the doorway of the little temple there invariably sat a blind beggar of the locality, named Chandu Surdas. He was a very quiet man—poor fellow—and eked out a precarious livelihood with the little doles that he got from the devotees visiting the temple. He was very miserable and at times was obliged to go without food for a day or two. Daily he used to pour out his heart in earnest prayer to Lord Ganesha.

"To that locality there came regularly, upon business visits, a certain rich stock-broker, Seth Murari Lall. He had amassed immense wealth through means both fair as well as foul. He had also lost heavily through horse-racing and gambling too. He was never satisfied with small transactions. The Sethji had heard from many about the great sanctity and mysterious power of Lord Ganesha of the little temple. Hence every time he visited the locality he used to stop his car, alight and make a formal circumambulation of the *sanctum sanctorum*. In return the Sethji desired a modest tenfold increase in his bank-roll.

"One evening he was returning from a neighbouring town after concluding an important business contract. It was late in the night and the Seth got down hurriedly before the Ganesha temple to do his usual circumambulation. But he heard strange voices from within the temple. He stopped to listen.

"A highly emotional devotee, Gajanan Dass, was sitting before the image of the Lord, sunk in deep

211

trance. Murari Lall had seen Gajanan Dass in this condition once or twice previously and also knew that whatever the latter uttered while in trance invariably came to pass with perfect accuracy. The devotee himself was totally unconscious of what he spoke.

"Now he was talking. The Seth listened intently. It seemed to be a conversation between two hidden voices. The first voice was of a divine, feminine tone.

" 'My son,' it said, 'do something for this poor beggar at thy door. This miserable Surdas is praying night and day for thy Grace. Do not be heedless to him any longer.'

"A second voice now replied: 'As the Mother of the universe and the consort of Maheshwara commands, tomorrow, before the stroke of twelve midday, I shall make this beggar the master of a lakh of rupees. His days of poverty and misery will end forever and he shall be put beyond all wants—else my name is not Ganesha.'

" 'Is this a promise, my son?'

" 'Yes, I have given my word.'

"Gajanan Dass lapsed into silence. His trance began to pass off. The Seth stopped to listen no more. He forgot to do his usual circumambulation too. He was fired with excitement. His crooked brain had conceived of a crafty plan to swindle the unknowing Chandu Surdas of the promised lakh of rupees.

"He did not return to his mansion that night but dozed in the car itself. He could hardly wait for dawn. The morning brought Surdas to his inevitable place by the temple door. As soon as he seated himself the Sethji hurried over and greeted him. He was trying to make his voice casual and unconcerned. The beggar was surprised at the unusual 'Namaste Bhagatji'.

Beggar Made a Millionaire

"'Look here!' the Seth continued, 'would you like to get a hundred rupees?' Poor Surdas nodded eagerly. 'Then, my good man, the one hundred rupees which I have decided to give away in charity today, will go to you. I have a small request, however. As a remembrance of our meeting I shall take for myself whatever you get as your daily collection in your bowl today. Your takings before midday will be mine.'

"Surdas agreed at once. He was readily willing to part with his insignificant daily pittance in return for a hundred rupees. Little did he dream of the wealth that was to come to him that day nor was he aware of the wicked scheme of the Seth to cheat him of his fortune with the paltry sum of one hundred rupees.

"The Seth took his seat in the inner court of the temple and commenced watching the beggar's bowl. Time passed and the day advanced. An occasional copper or two and a few pice were all that fell into the bowl. The beggar did not mind anything for he was to get a veritable fortune of one hundred rupees that day. But the Seth began to fume. Midday was fast drawing nigh. Dark thoughts arose in his mind. Was the temple Deity about to cheat him? What! was Murari Lall going to be thus trifled with? God or no God, he, Murari Lall was going to have his lakh by hook or crook.

"It was 11.30. The Seth's temper got the better of him. He was getting deeply chagrined. He arose and swiftly entered the inner *sanctum*. He was wrathful. On approaching the sacred image he brandished his clenched fist before its face. He swore at it, calling it 'liar', 'deceiver', 'boaster'. There stood the idol in front of him, as impassive as ever, with the same calm, inscrutable expression upon its dark, smooth, stony face. The money-mad Seth lost his temper and with a

213

shout of anger delivered one hard blow upon the elephant trunk of Ganesha.

"Lo! the next moment a truly awesome thing happened. As soon as the clenched fist of the Seth struck the trunk of the Deity, the serpentine curve of the trunk suddenly straightened out with a lightning movement and wound itself tightly around his arm. The Seth's hand became imprisoned in a vice-like grip. He was seized with terror. He struggled to free himself. He tried desperately to wrench his hand free. The more he tugged, the tighter the grip grew. He was pulled nearer to the idol. The image now caught hold of his hands with its four arms and the trunk encircled itself around his throat.

"A voice now spoke and said, 'Murari Lall, if you want to save your life, send thy driver to thy house and immediately get one lakh of rupees. The money must be in that beggar's bowl by twelve. Quick! Hurry up lest the midday be passed! He should get it before midday. I always keep my promise. My word is never in vain.'

"The mention of giving away one lakh staggered the wretched Seth. He now began to plead hard with the Deity. He had no intention of ever parting with his dear money. But the grip on his neck tightened. The bones of his hands felt as though they were being crushed. He began to pant. In a hoarse voice he called out to the driver. After five minutes of calling the driver appeared from the lane outside. The Seth whispered to him to come closer. Then in urgent tones he requested the servant to hurry home at once and instruct his cashier, Ramniklal, to come to the temple with one lakh of rupees.

" 'Say it is a matter of life and death,' the terrified Seth added.

214

Beggar Made a Millionaire

"The driver hurried away. Within half an hour he returned with the trembling cashier clutching the money bag with the required amount. By this time the Seth was in the throes of terror and agony. He gasped out, 'Give the lakh of rupees to the man sitting at the door. Take him home and hand the amount to his wife. Do it before the neighbours as witness. Hurry! Do it at once!'

"The cashier was struck dumb. But the urgency of the Seth was unmistakable. When the money was being handed over to the wife of Chandu Surdas, the coils of the trunk around the neck of Murari Lall loosened and his hands were freed. He sank to the floor at the feet of the sacred image.

"Thinking that the master was overtaken by some strange illness, the driver lifted him and took him to the waiting car and drove straight home. Thus did the Lord bring to pass His Will and turned the blind beggar into a rich man."

The strange Sadhu paused at the end of the even stranger narrative.

"And," he added, "I can vouch for the truth of this occurrence. I am Murari Lall, the Seth!"

The group of listeners gasped. The monk walked away and disappeared before they could recover from their astonishment.

God can make and unmake things in the twinkling of an eye. Know this and be humble. Nothing is of any avail before His Divine Will. To deny it is sheer folly. Rather choose to attune thyself to His Will. Then you will find blessedness and bliss blossoming forth in this very life.

67

GURU BHAKTI

SANKAR WENT to Swami Prakashanand for initiation. He told the Swamiji, "O Maharaj! I have come to your holiness for initiation. I must realise the Atman quickly. I want to become your most devoted disciple also. What should I do to realise my Self soon and become your most devoted disciple? Certainly I will obey thy commands. Kindly guide me. I am suppliant to thee."

Swami Prakashanandaji said, "O Sankar! I am much pleased with you as you wish to realise the Truth quickly. I shall certainly guide you. You are very dear to me as you seem to be a first class type of aspirant. Give me your body, mind and soul. That is all. You can then become my devoted disciple."

"Is that all?" asked Sankar. "From this moment I give thee my body, mind and soul. Kindly initiate me."

Swami Prakashanandaji gave him the Mantra and spiritual instructions. Sankar was doing Japa of the Guru Mantra regularly and following the spiritual instructions of his Guru.

One day the Swamiji Maharaj wished to have some mangoes for his use. He could not get them in the bazaar. He came to know that his disciple Sankar had plenty of mangoes in his garden. He sent a servant to bring some mangoes from his disciple's garden.

Sankar sent word through the servant, "Tell my Guru that he wanted my body, mind and soul. I have already given them to him. What more does he want? I cannot give him any mangoes. They are for the sole use of myself, my wife and children."

Look at the behaviour of this most devoted disciple! Such disciples are in abundance these days. They talk a lot. They write a lot. They say, "We have given up our lives and everything to our Guru. He is our revered father, Guru, preceptor; he is our God. He is our worshipful Master, our all-in-all." When they are put to the test their devotion evaporates like ether. Out of curiosity for getting some powers they will approach a Yogi or Sannyasin. When they find that they cannot get any Siddhis, they run to another Guru. Every year they will seek new Gurus. They themselves will not do any rigorous spiritual practice. They wish that the Guru should perform some miracle and by this miracle they should acquire psychic powers and Self-realisation quickly.

Vimal went to Swami Paramananda for initiation and said to him, "O revered Swamiji! make me your disciple."

Swami Paramananda replied, "My dear Vimal, stay with me for one year. Let me know your virtues and capacities. Let me study your character and nature."

Vimal agreed. He reluctantly did a little service to his Guru for two months.

One day the Swamiji called his disciple. "Vimal, there is no grass for the cow today. Kindly go to the neighbouring fields and bring some grass."

Vimal replied, "Guruji, I am not able to walk today.

There is a big thorn in my right foot."

The Swamiji allowed him to take rest that day.

After ten days, Swamiji said, "Vimal, today is Ekadasi. Our camphor is exhausted. Go to the bazaar and purchase some camphor."

"Guru Maharaj, I have a very severe headache today. It has been troubling me since yesterday. My head is reeling. I will faint and fall down if I walk as far as the bazaar."

Guruji said, "Vimal, take rest for a couple of days."

After a week, Swamiji again said to Vimal, "Vimal, how is your health? I think you are feeling quite fit today. Can you bring a pot of water from the Ganges?"

Vimal replied, "Guruji, my headache is gone but I am suffering from a very bad sprain of my right ankle. I cannot walk even a few yards. The pain is unbearable."

"Vimal, give some hot fomentation. Take plenty of rest for three or four days."

After another ten days, the Swamiji said to Vimal, "There are some fruits and sweetmeats for you in the corner room. Kindly take them."

Vimal replied, "Guru Maharaj, for how long can I disobey you? I feel ashamed. I will obey you now. I am quite well today."

He ran to the room and at once polished off the fruits and sweetmeats!

Prakash went to Benares in search of a Guru. He roamed about hither and thither and met several Sannyasins. At last he came to Swami Vishuddananda, a Sannyasin of very great reputation.

Prakash made prostrations and said, "Venerable Guru, kindly instruct me. I long for the attainment of Brahma Gyana."

Guru Bhakti

The Swamiji replied, "Stay in my Ashram for two or three years. I shall initiate you into the mysteries of Kaivalya. I shall explain to you the right significance of the *Tat Twam Asi* Mahavakya."

Prakash stayed in the Ashram for six months. He studied the *Vivekachudamani, Atma Bodha* and *Tattwa Bodha.*

One day he went to his Guru and said, "Revered Guruji, I have a great doubt. It has been tormenting me for a long time. Your noble self alone is the proper person to dispel it."

The Swamiji said, "Prakash, what is your doubt? I shall clear it."

"Swamiji, who is superior, the Guru or the disciple?"

Swamiji replied, "Guru is superior."

Prakash said, "Swamiji, will you then make me a Guru? I would rather be a Guru than a disciple, because the Guru is superior."

There was a very learned man named Krishna Shastry in Rameshwaram. He had a disciple called Ram. One day Krishna Shastry's box, which contained the image of Lord Krishna, was missing. He asked his disciple, "O Ram, where did you keep the Puja box?"

Ram replied, "I kept the Puja box in the place where I performed Puja."

The learned Shastry again asked, "Ram, where did you perform the Puja?"

"In the place where the Puja box was kept."

What a pertinent reply Ram gave his Guru!

Disciples like Vimal, Prakash and Ram can be found in abundance at all times. Many aspirants stay with their Gurus for six months and then become Gurus themselves like Prakash and wander about aimlessly.

Inspiring Stories

No disciple wants to serve his Guru with faith and sincerity. There is no better purifier than the constant service of one's own Guru. By constant contact the disciple imbibes the virtues of his Guru. He is moulded gradually.

68

THE YOUNG MAN AND THE PUNDIT

ONE EVENING, a young man was walking along the banks of a river with a woman. He had a bottle in his hand. Sometimes he carried the woman on his back. After walking a short distance the woman sat on the ground. The young man also sat at her side and shampooed her legs. He drank from the contents of the bottle.

A Brahmin Pundit of the village, who was also taking a walk along the banks of the river, was closely watching the actions of the young man. He hurried to the village and said to the headman, "A young, immoral man is drinking wine publicly. He is keeping the company of a young woman also. He is doing immoral actions openly. He is setting a bad example. He should be driven out at once from this place."

The headman took some people along with him to drive the couple away. As there was heavy rain and also hail-storm, they stopped in a shed and watched the actions of the young man.

The young man again drank of the contents of the bottle and shampooed the legs of the woman. The headman also thought that the young man was an immoral wreck who was addicted to drink.

A boat in the river suddenly capsized on account of the heavy storm. The passengers were about to be drowned. Without hesitation the young man jumped into the river and saved all of them by bringing them to the shore one by one. The headman and the Pundit did not stir from the shed. They were all the while laughing and joking amongst themselves.

The rain stopped. The headman came to the young man and asked, "How is it that you are drinking liquor openly and doing immoral actions in public? Who is this woman?"

The young man replied, "I have already walked thirty miles today. I have to cover a distance of ten miles more before I reach my village. I was very tired and thirsty. Today it is very hot. This bottle contains pure Ganges water. This woman is my mother. She is suffering from heart disease and acute rheumatism. She cannot walk. I carry her on my back. I shampoo her legs as she suffers from unbearable pain."

The Brahmin Pundit hung his heads in shame. The village headman was stunned. He thought within himself: "I had formed a very hasty opinion of this noble young man. I did not use my common sense. What a great mistake I committed! Look at his sympathetic heart! How brave he is! He at once jumped into the river and saved the lives of the passengers. We were only talking and joking. How politely he talks. This lady is in acute agony."

He scolded the Brahmin Pundit severely and at once arranged for a bullock cart and sent the mother and son to their village. He gave them plenty of milk to refresh themselves.

You should always think well before you come to a conclusion. Appearances are not always to be trusted.

The Young Man and the Pundit

You should possess keen discernment, good power of judgment and common sense. You must have all the correct facts and detailed particulars before you take any action in a matter. You must not be carried away by the false reports and wild rumours of mischief-mongers. Mere book learning will not help much. It will make you arrogant and proud.

69

WHAT GOD DOES IS FOR THE BEST

ONCE THERE was a great king named Vikram, famous
for his bravery and lion-hunting. His chief minister,
Ajit, was well known for his wisdom, honesty, loyalty
and able administration. He had great devotion to
Lord Siva. He was a man of strong character and high
morals, always depending on the Lord. He had intense
faith in the saying: "Whatever God does is for the best."

King Vikram had a brother named Banbir. He was
very intelligent but cunning. He was a devil in the garb
of a humble brother and was inclined to mischief. He
was always secretly scheming to dethrone his brother.

Banbir always considered Ajit as a great and only
obstacle, because his many plans against his brother
failed, due to the alertness, dexterity and sincerity of
Ajit. Ajit suspected Banbir, but in the absence of sub-
stantial proof, never uttered a single word against him.

One day, a finger of the king got cut by accident.
When the king told Ajit about it, the latter respectfully
said, "Whatever God does is always for our good. This
accident is also for our good."

The king felt this to be an insult and got enraged.
Thinking this a good opportunity, Banbir whispered
some words so tactfully that made the king lose his

temper. He thereupon ordered the chief minister to be put into jail. The king's order was obeyed immediately. Ajit just smiled at the incident and said, "It is all for the good."

A few days later the king started on a hunting trip, agreeing with a programme chalked out by his younger brother, Banbir. While hunting, he entered into the dense part of the forest, leaving his companions far behind in pursuit of his quarry. He lay down beneath a shady tree waiting for his companions to arrive. Due to tiredness, he was soon overpowered by sleep. A loud roar suddenly awakened him. He saw a furious lion approaching. Finding no way of escape he closed his eyes and lay motionless on the ground, holding his breath. The lion came and sniffed at its victim. As soon as it saw and smelt the injured finger, it turned and went away. The king observed this and now realised that his injured finger was responsible for his life having been saved. He felt very sorry for putting Ajit behind bars. He immediately got up and hastened towards the hunting camp.

Vikram had expected that his brother Banbir and his men would search for him, but he was disappointed. It was late at night when the king reached the camp. He found five soldiers talking in hushed tones around a fire. He suspected some mischief and hid himself in a bush nearby so that he could hear them clearly.

Their conversation disclosed the whole secret of the conspiracy, which was made by Banbir to murder him and Ajit and become the king himself.

Instead of entering the fenced boundary of the camp the king left for his capital at once. As soon as he reached his palace he sent for his commander-in-chief and ordered him to attack the camp without delay with a troop of reliable soldiers. He ordered that Banbir and his followers be arrested.

The next morning Ajit was brought to the Durbar before the king. As soon as he entered the court the king ordered that he be unchained. He embraced Ajit with love and joy and apologised for his past mistake. He asked him to assume the position of the chief minister once again and rewarded him generously.

The king then narrated the whole story of his hunting, his meeting with the lion and the conspiracy of his brother. After finishing the story, he asked Ajit to explain how his imprisonment also was for the good.

Ajit laughed and replied, "I was intending to construct a big and beautiful temple for Lord Siva in my village, but could not do so for lack of money. Now the reward so kindly given will enable me to fulfil my long-felt desire. The Lord always does everything for the best. His ways are very mysterious and very difficult for us to understand."

70

GLORY OF GLORIFICATION

THERE LIVED in a certain village in India an old woman, along with her sons and daughters-in-law. As she was penniless, no one treated her well and her daughters-in-law constantly quarrelled with her.

One day the old woman felt disgusted with her unhappy life and quietly left the house. She walked on and on. As she reached a dense forest, she met *summer* in the form of a beautiful woman, who asked her, "Tell me, mother, how do you like me?"

The old woman replied with a smile, "About you, O sweet thing? You are the best of seasons. After the biting, cold weather, we welcome you with open arms. How we enjoy a moonlit night in summer and love to inhale the cool, fresh, fragrant morning breeze! You come and life comes along with joy. Ice and ice-cream and refreshing cool drinks are all your gifts. You are the queen of seasons. I love you so."

Hearing this, *summer* was immensely pleased. She thanked the old woman and gave her gold worth thousands as a token of her love.

As the woman went a little further, she met the *rainy season* in the form of a sweet girl dressed in a green *sari*. She saluted the old woman an asked her how she liked her. The old woman praised her in glorious terms, saying she was the beauty of life, that without her life would be barren, dull and dreary. In the rainy season the whole of Nature is rejuvenated. Brooks murmur and gardens smile. The children sing and dance in joy.

"Even old men wink and whistle. Poets get inspiration from thee. Picnics and parties are thy presents, O enchanting princess! The world welcomes thee with love and gratitude."

The *rainy season* was greatly pleased and elated. She presented the old woman with a purse heavy with many precious gems.

The old woman was well pleased at her good fortune. As she paced on a little further, she met *winter*, solemnly dressed in white. She greeted the old woman and asked her how she liked her. The old woman praised her also as best as she could and in all sincerity. So *winter* too presented her with a huge sum and went her way very pleased.

The old woman was now in good cheer and thought of returning home. On reaching her family she related the whole story to her children. As she was now rich, she was loved and respected by all.

Now there was another poor old woman in the neighbourhood, who was also a victim of her children's ill-treatment. She heard all about this woman's good fortune and thought of following suit. So she also left the house and went on her way. She too met the seasons one after the other. But the woman disparaged them all in the most unbecoming terms. So the three seasons beat her. The unhappy old woman, sorrow stricken and sorely starved, had to return home and spend her days more miserably than before.

71

AKBAR AND THE BEGGAR

BADSHAH AKBAR held a great feast in which many thousands participated. There was sumptuous feeding of many thousands upon thousands of rich and poor.

When a batch of people sat down in the palace hall to take their food, all of them except one sang the praises of the Badshah and shouted at the top of their voices—"Akbar Badshah ki jai."

Akbar, who was watching the proceedings from his balcony, sent for the man who did not take part in this chanting and shouting.

"Tell him that he shall not be gven food here. Unless he joins in the chorus of my praise and unless he says, 'Akbar Badshah ki jai', he shall not be allowed even to enter the palace. Drag him out and throw him out of the gates."

The Badshah's orders were instantly and ruthlessly carried out.

That night Badshah Akbar tossed about restlessly in bed. He could not sleep. Some mysterious voice was uttering the words: "Akbar, though I am the Almighty God whose glories are sung by millions of wise men, I do not deny my blessings and protection to even the lowliest of the low, the poorest of the poor and the most wicked of the wicked ones who abuse me, who deny My very existence. Will you then refuse to feed the man who did not sing your praise? That man is a great saint and he is My devotee. He need not sing your praise, but if you feed him you will be blessed."

Akbar could not believe his ears. Then the voice steadily grew in intensity and pitch and the entire bedroom began resounding with the words. At last Akbar was convinced that it was the voice of God.

At dawn, he sent all his messengers in search of the poor man. When the man arrived, Akbar fell at his feet and asked for pardon.

The saint smiled and said, "Badshah, you have no need to ask for pardon. God can never be offended. So also His devotees—they are free from wrath. You are blessed, for what you did gave you an opportunity to listen to His voice and learn a lesson from Him."

TREASURE BENEATH THE PILLOW

THE STRANGER was happy that he had won the confidence of the wealthy pilgrim. The latter was travelling alone and had thousands of rupees with him. The stranger felt sure that one day or the other he would be able to steal the money.

Every morning, in the presence of the stranger, the pilgrim would count all the money he had. All day long it would be in his pocket. He had no box in which to lock it. Yet, when at night the stranger searched for it, he could not find it. This went on night after night. The stranger searched for the money in the pilgrim's belongings, underneath his pillow and bed, everywhere. He could not find the money. Yet, sure enough the next morning it would be there in the hands of the pilgrim.

This mysterious game went on for over a week. The stranger was frightened. He thought that the pilgrim might be a magician or a Yogi with powers. So he confessed his evil intentions and asked the pilgrim, "Where did you keep the money all the time during the night? How did I miss it in my search?"

The pilgrim laughed heartily and said, "My friend, I knew your intentions. Therefore I used to keep the money underneath *your* pillow at night. You never looked for it there!"

The stranger is the wayward mind full of desires. The pilgrim is God. The treasure is the bliss of the Atman. The wicked mind wants to get happiness and seeks for it in sensual objects. It is not found there. Finally it abandons its evil intentions and approaches God in a spirit of surrender. God reveals that the happiness was within all the time, in the Self, and not outside.

THE HUMOROUS FRUIT-SELLER

ONCE A RAJAH held a magnificent feast. He invited many other Rajahs, landlords and officers. He obtained plenty of grapes, oranges, apples and various kinds of vegetables and sweetmeats. But he could not obtain any good mangoes.

Just at that time a fruit-seller was passing along the road in front of the palace with plenty of good mangoes. The gatekeeper called him and said, "Today, Rajah Sahib will purchase all your mangoes as there is a big feast. But you will have to give me half of your profit, then only will I allow you to enter the palace."

The fruit-seller was at first a little hesitant but finally consented. He was a very intelligent and humorous man. He entered the compound of the palace.

The Rajah Sahib purchased all the mangoes and asked the fruit-seller, "How much money do you want?"

The fruit-seller replied, "Rajah Sahib, I do not want money. Please beat me one hundred times with a stick."

The Rajah was struck with amazement. He said, "Take a generous amount as payment. Your mangoes are very delicious. How can I beat you when you

233

have given me the fruit I was so urgently in need of? I have to offer you special thanks."

But the fruit-seller again said, "No, no. You must only beat me a hundred times. I will then be immensely pleased and satisfied."

The Rajah Sahib ordered his peon to beat him one hundred times mildly. The peon beat him fifty times and was about to raise the stick for the fifty-first time, when the fruit-seller exclaimed, "Stop now! Stop now! I have a partner. You will have to beat him also fifty times."

The Rajah was quite astonished. What sort of funny, humorous man this is! He asked, "Who is your partner?"

The fruit-seller replied, "When I wanted to enter the compound of the palace, your gatekeeper wanted me to share half of my profit with him. So he must get his share of fifty beatings."

The Rajah Sahib immediately sent for the gate-keeper and asked the peon to thrash him fifty times severely and dismiss him from service at once. The fruit-seller received rich presents for his honest dealings.

A man of honesty is always to be respected. Honesty brings its own reward. Honesty is not only the best policy, it is also a sublime virtue. An honest man is always successful in any kind of work. People place great faith in him.

A greedy man is hated by his own people. He always leads a restless, discontented and miserable life. He is like a leach or vulture. He sucks the blood of others. He exploits them. He takes recourse to tricks and any kind of foul means in order to obtain money. Money is his goal. Money is his God. He does not hesitate even to commit murder for the sake of money. Greed clouds understanding and makes a man blind. Selfishness, cheating, double-dealing, diplomacy and hypocrisy are the constant companions of greed. The root cause of war is greed. It is the pet child of Maya or ignorance. It is like a chameleon. It ever assumes various colours or forms. There is greed for money, greed for psychic powers, for Gurudom, disciples and Ashrams.

Destroy greed through charity, Satsang and honesty. You will then enjoy supreme peace and bliss.

SHADOW AND SUBSTANCE

A MAN DID not want his shadow. He discovered that it always came along with him, haunting him every second. He said to himself: "I will bury this shadow. I must rid myself of it."

He dug a deep pit. He looked into it and found his shadow at the bottom of the pit. He was exceedingly pleased. He made haste to fill the pit with mud. As he shoved mud into it, he found to his dismay that the shadow was coming up. Quickly he filled the pit, but the shadow was again on top of it! He gave up the task!

He now wanted to run away from his shadow. He began to run—but ran away from the sun, in the opposite direction. He now found that his shadow was running ahead of him and he could not overtake it, however fast he ran.

He then turned round and began to run towards the sun. He was happy now that he was able to overtake his shadow; he was running ahead of it. But no, he still could not get rid of it.

Finally, he lay down, facing the sky. He turned to his left and right to see if the shadow was anywhere. No, he had lost it! Now he slept peacefully!

Even so, "I"-ness and "mine"-ness follow man every-

236

where, dogging his footsteps. Egoism comes on top of all that the aspirant does to bury it and destroy it. It runs ahead of him as he starts running away from it. Pride of learning, pride of austerities, pride of service, pride of being humble—it takes any number of forms. When he starts running towards God, then it is left behind. When he surrenders himself to God totally, it is completely vanquished. He is now at peace with himself. He is free from cares, worries and anxieties. He enjoys unbroken bliss and joy.

THE SADHAK'S PATH

SUBODH AND VIVEK are receiving scriptural education at the Ashram of their Guru, a Sannyasin. They are nearing the completion of their studies. The austere life they had led in the Gurukula, the Satsang they enjoyed with the saintly Mahatma, their Guru, and the theoretical knowledge of the *Shastras*, had generated in them an aspiration to lead the life of renunciation, to dedicate themselves to whole time Sadhana for Self-realisation.

On a Guru Purnima day they approach the Guru with their request to be "initiated".The Guru expresses his joy at their aspiration, and whilst congratulating them on their discrimination, counsels a little caution in taking such a drastic step blindly.

"Sannyas is a blazing fire and you should prepare yourself well before embracing it. You have as yet had no knowledge or experience of the world. The spirit of dispassion that you have now got from a study of scriptural texts and by remaining in this pure and holy atmosphere, may or may not be real; it may or may not last till the end of your life. At some later period in your life, temptations might assail you and lead you astray. Therefore a little experience of the true nature of the world will fortify your dispassion, which would then be unshakable.

"Today is the auspicious Guru Purnima day. Now go out into the world. Roam about the country for one year. You will learn many things. The world is your best teacher. Keep your eyes and ears open—learn and learn. But keep your mouth shut. Do not take part in worldly activities. Just watch and learn. As far as possible live in the company of the wise. If this is not possible, live in seclusion as much as possible. Then come back after a year. You will gain rich experience during this one year and I also will be reassured that your dispassion is real and unshakable.

"May the blessings of my Gurudev grant you wisdom and strength!"

The two young men leave the Ashram after bowing to their Guru.

IN THE DULLARD'S DURBAR

Hearing that the Rajah of a nearby state had a number of learned men in his Durbar, the two aspirants go there. They are very well received by the Rajah. The court Pundit is giving expositions of scriptures for the enlightenment of the people who attend the Durbar. But the Rajah himself is interested only in fun and frolic and so takes no pains to learn.

A learned scoundrel is tempted by the Rajah's ignorance to play upon his love of the vulgar and to earn a fortune. He goes to the Durbar and boasts of his extensive learning and deep wisdom.

"Give me proof of your learning," says the Rajah.

"Maharaj! you must have surely heard the well-known Sloka: "Shuklambaradharam Vishnum Shashi-Varnam Chaturbhujam Prasanna Vadanam Dhyaayet

Sarva Vighnopashaantaye". What is it that is referred
to by this Sloka?"

"Surely, Lord Maha Vishnu," replies the Rajah.

"No, no. You are wrong. It refers to a glittering rupee-
coin. The rupee-coin is white, it pervades the entire
world and never stays at one place with anyone. It is of
the form of the full moon and has forty-four annas. It
removes all our obstacles and makes every person
happy."

"You seem to be far more learned than our court
Pundit."

"What doubt is there!" replies the scoundrel.

The Rajah promptly drives away the wise court
Pundit and appoints this imposter in his place. The
cunning imposter amasses wealth and one day takes
leave of the Rajah.

In the meantime the court Pundit goes to the assembly of wise men and bewails his fate. A senior Pundit
volunteers to teach the Rajah a lesson. He goes over to
him in disguise and boasts that there is not a man
more learned than himself in the whole world.

"Give us some proof of your wisdom."

"Maharaj, you might have heard of the Sloka: 'Shuklambaradharam . . . Shaantaye'. Do you know the
meaning?"

"Yes, yes. My first court Pundit said it meant Lord
Vishnu. The second one whom I appointed said that it
meant a rupee-coin."

"Both of them are wrong. It refers to *dahi-bada*, you
know—the *bada* soaked in curd."

"That seems to be interesting, Punditji. How do you
explain it?"

"The rupee-coin is not clothed in white, but the
dahi-bada is. It is actually clothed in curd. It is our

240

protector. It is of the form of the full moon. It is eaten by all the four castes. Its very thought makes one joyous. One should therefore meditate upon *dahi-bada* and eat it regularly."

"Wonderful, Punditji! The other two people are surely wrong. Luckily my second court Pundit has gone home on leave. I appoint you as my third court Pundit."

"Well, that man came here to loot you and he has succeeded," said the Pundit, and then revealed his identity.

"Do you recognise me? I am the friend of your first court Pundit. He was a wise man. His interpretation of the Sloka alone is correct. The Sloka refers to Maha Vishnu alone. I gave it a twist only in order to please you. But Maharaj, this won't do. So long as you are ignorant yourself, you will be a pawn in the hands of every passing cunning man. Become wise. Recall the first court Pundit. Learn the *Shastras* yourself. Then you will be able to judge for yourself. No one can then deceive you."

The Rajah was convinced.

Subodh and Vivek learn their first lesson and move on.

THE FOUR DACOITS

As they walk along the jungle path early in the morning, they find a Sadhu hurrying along the path.

"Death, worse than death! I am not afraid of a lion or tiger. But this money, oh! it is the greatest destroyer in the world."

Puzzled, the two young men move on. They find four dacoits with two bags of money, laughing and joking. The chief feels hungry. He sends two of his companions to fetch some food. While the two are away, the chief and his deputy gloat over the prospect of a rich share of the loot. Satan enters their hearts; the thought occurs to them that if they do away with the other two, they could get a larger share of the money.

At the same time the two who have gone to the bazaar get the very same idea—if the chief and his deputy are killed, they could get all the money to be shared between them. They mix poison in the food that they fetch from the bazaar.

When they return to the hide-out they place the food in front of the chief and the deputy. Suddenly the chief and his friend spring upon the other two and murder them. With doubly gladdened hearts at the prospect of a greater share of the money they fall to eating the food. The poison kills them also.

Subodh and Vivek watch this tragedy and pass on their way, musing: "Lord Yama is nothing before this killer of the very soul of man—money!"

THE SHASTRI AND THE GENTLEMAN

On another day, Subodh and Vivek are taking rest at a rest-house. On the road in front of the rest-house two friends are talking. One is a Shastri and the other a fashionable man. They were obviously once class-mates.

"O Shastriji! where are you going to?"

"To Calcutta to attend the holy Dharma Sammelan. Where are *you* going to?"

'I am also going to Calcutta," replied the friend.

"To attend the Sammelan?"

"O you and your Dharma Sammelan! Do you think I am also an antique like you? No, I am going to attend the International Film Festival. Why don't you give up your old-fashioned outlook and enjoy life? It is only on account of people like you that India is so backward. Look at America and the other Western nations. They are advancing. But you are clinging to your old, outdated traditions. Time is changing. Your views also should change. When your religion, philosophy and outlook on life grow old, you should throw them away."

"H'm! How is your father? How old is he?"

"He is all right. He is eighty-five."

"Old enough to be thrown away, I think."

"What rubbish you are talking, Shastriji?"

The gentleman goes forward to slap Shastriji, who escapes in time.

The two aspirants watch this in wonderment and move on.

BLINDED BY CATARACT, BLINDED BY ENVY

When Subodh suffers from coal-dust in his eyes, the two Sadhakas go to the local eye hospital. The doctor is away. They find five eye patients there. They have been operated upon for cataract and have been instructed to lie quietly without moving their heads. Their eyes are heavily bandaged.

Something suddenly startles one of the patients. In an automatic reflex action, he jumps up. Then he begins to think: "My God! the doctor told me that if I even moved my head, my eyesight will be lost for ever. I have sat up. Surely my eyesight is gone. But why should the man lying next to me be all right. If I am to be blind, he might as well be blind too."

He rudely shakes the next man. He too sits up. In this manner all the patents are up and quarrelling.

The doctor arrives and regrets their action.

"You have not only lost your eyesight but have ruined the eyesight of others too. What a foolish thing you have done!

STATE MOURNING FOR THE DONKEY

Subodh and Vivek continue their journey and come to a barber's shop. They find several people waiting to have a shave. A rich social leader of he place also comes in. While he is having a shave, his washerman passes along the road weeping and wailing aloud.

"What is the matter? Why are you weeping?" asks the rich man.

"What shall I say, Sethji? Gandharvasen is dead."

"Who is Gandharvasen?"

The washerman is not in a mood nor has he the sense to reply calmly.

"Gandharvasen was a great Paropakari. How can I live without him?" and he goes away. The socal leader thinks that Gandharvasen is a great Mahatma.

"I too should mourn for the Mahatma," he says and shaves his head as a sign of his grief.

As he is returning home he meets the inspector of police on the way. The inspector is surprised to see the mournful face of the leader and questions him.

The Seth replies, "A great calamity, inspector Sahib! Gandharvasen, the Mahatma, is dead."

The inspector wants to follow the example of the Seth and he too has his head shaved.

When later in the day he goes to see the Rajah, he is questioned and tells the Rajah, "Gandharvasen, the Mahatma, is dead."

The Rajah declares state mourning for the saint and himself puts on his mourning dress.

The queen is intrigued by all this. She asks the

Rajah, "Who is this Gandharvasen? Is he such a great Mahatma that you should declare state mourning?"

The Rajah sends for the inspector and questions him; the inspector pleads ignorance and brings the Seth; the Seth also does not know and calls for the washerman.

The washerman cries out bitterly, "Gandharvasen was truly a great soul."

When the Rajah asks, "Where did the Mahatma live?" the washerman is dismayed and says, "Who says that he was a Mahatma? Gandharvasen was my donkey. Oh! how can I live without my donkey?" And he wails again.

The Rajah gets furious and rebukes the Seth and the police inspector.

Subodh and Vivek, who had been silently watching the whole episode, laugh at the stupid way in which the blind follow the blind. They go on their way.

THE STORY OF THE BHAKTA

A Satsang is in progress in Rishikesh. Subodh and Vivek join the gathering. The Guru is discoursing on Sadhana and Jnana.

"Beloved aspirants! Bhakti is the greatest thing in the world. A Bhakta is equal, if not superior to the Lord Himself. I will illustrate this with a story.

"There arose a question once: 'Who is the greatest person in the universe?'

"Earth first answered, 'It is I, because I hold the entire humanity, besides all the plants and beasts and all the sacred places and holy rivers.'

"Adisesha, the Great Serpent could not remain silent. 'I am greater than Earth for I hold Earth itself on my hood.'

"Lord Siva gave a hearty laugh that shook the universe, and said, 'And I wear this serpent around my neck; so I am greater than Adisesha.'

"Mount Kailas now got its turn and said, 'I hold Lord Siva and His entire family on the crown of my head, so I am greater than Lord Siva Himself.'

"Ravana of Lanka roared with his ten mouths. 'I uprooted the Kailas with my superhuman strength; I am greater than Kailas.'

"Vali, the great monkey, came forward and said, 'This ten-headed beast I caught in my arm-pit and gave to my son as a plaything. I am infinitely greater than Ravana.'

"Now it was Sri Rama's turn. 'Did I not kill Vali with one arrow? I am greater than all the others.'

"A humble devotee of Lord Rama, who was totally immersed in Bhava Samadhi, got up from meditation when Sri Rama spoke, and quietly added, 'And this Sri Rama is my captive. I have bound Him with the chords of my supreme devotion and imprisoned Him in my heart. How can my prisoner be greater than myself?'

"No one dared to contradict the devotee. No one came forward to claim superiority over him. It was agreed on all hands that he was indeed the greatest of all, greater than even the Lord Himself. Such is the glory of Bhakti or supreme devotion to the Lord.

"Due to ignorance man identifies himself with the body, mind and Prana. Listen to this amusing story of a deluded man.

"A man addicted to taking intoxicating drugs used to carry the mortar and pestle with which the drug was to be prepared. He had it tied to his waist. One day as he was walking along the banks of a river the lure of the drug made him halt beneath a tree. He prepared his drug, gulped it down and then, after tying the mortar and pestle to his waist, went into the drunkard's slumber.

"Another lover of the drug happened to pass that way. He carried his own supply with him and was eager to have it. But he did not have the mortar and pestle. He saw these tied to the waist of the sleeping drunkard. Quietly he removed them from the slumberer's waist, prepared the drug and enjoyed it. In his intoxication he could not remember that the instruments belonged to the other man and so he tied them around his own waist. After a while the first drunkard woke up and his eyes fell upon the mortar and pestle tied to the waist of the second man.

"He began to reflect: 'The mortar and pestle were tied to *my* waist. If that be the truth, then I must be that sleeping person. But I was wearing a black shawl and I find a red shawl on that person. If I am the man with the black shawl I must be this person. Oh! I am confused. Am I the man with the mortar and pestle or the man with the black shawl?'

"He could not solve this riddle until the intoxication passed off. Then he realised that he was unnecessarily worrying over superficial extraneous factors which did not at all belong to his own self and were mere cloaks and possessions.

"When a man has forgotten his real identity, and through wrong identification with the body and mind suffers grief and pain, the Guru awakens him to the nature of his real Self; that is the end of ignorance and its countless evil effects. Listen to this story of a washerman and a lion.

"A washerman was instructing his son who was washing clothes: 'My son, it is nearing nightfall. Get ready to return home. I am very much afraid of night. I am not afraid of tigers or lions, but night makes me sick with fright.'

"A lion that was hiding in a bush nearby heard the remarks of the washerman. It mused within itself: 'What kind of being is this "night"? Judging from the remarks of this man, it must be much superior in strength to me even, the king of the jungle.'

"Fear of the unknown night crept into the heart of the beast.

"The washerman was searching for his donkey which had not returned home that evening. In the dark he could not see clearly, but he espied an animal crouching in the bush. It was the lion. He thought it was his donkey and gave it a couple of good blows with his stick. The lion confirmed its fear. 'This must be the mighty night. Thank God I am let off with only two blows!' It got up and followed the man to his house. The washerman did not notice that it was a lion and simply tied it in the yard and went to sleep. The lion was greatly worried.

"Early in the morning, the washerman put a big load of clothes on the back of the lion. It was still dark and so he could not discover that it was a lion. He led it to the river. The poor lion followed him meekly. Another lion met this lion on the way and laughed. 'What is this that you are doing? Are you not ashamed that, being a lion, you are doing the work of a donkey?. Throw away that burden and come with me.'

But this lion would not listen. 'Brother, you don't know what this terrible creature—night—did to me. Keep quiet or it will beat you also.'

"The second lion laughed at this lion's foolishness. 'Look, just roar once and see what happens.'

"It did so. The washerman looked back and in the dim light of dawn saw the lion. He bolted away without even caring for the clothes! The two lions walked away into the forest.

"When the Guru thus opens the eyes of the aspirant, delusion vanishes and with it fear and grief too."

Subodh and Vivek rejoice at this opportunity given to them to attend the Satsang. They recollect that Guru Purnima is nearing and so return to the Ashram of their Guru.

The Guru explains to them the moral of all the incidents.

Before reforming others, reform yourself. Before attempting to judge others, acquire the highest knowledge yourself. Then only will you know what is good and what is evil. You cannot know by proxy. You have to do your Sadhana yourself. Become wise yourself.

You have understood the untold misery that money brings upon man. Money is the most powerful weapon of Maya; the other is lust. Maya has put a few drops of sweetness into a potful of the most virulent poisons—wealth and lust. Man, tempted by those few drops of sweetness, drinks the poison and courts endless suffering.

Remember that death kills only your body. Lust and wealth go much deeper and blacken your very soul. It takes several lives to retrieve the purity of your soul. Lust and greed make you an animal. And God, finding that you have not deserved the glorious human birth He has granted you, throws you into lower births, to suffer in the filth of sense-indulgence until His mercy and Grace again grant you a human birth. If you wish to tread the path of goodness, shun lust and greed.

Do not belittle our ancient spiritual culture. Modern materialistic civilisation has brought nothing but disharmony, misery, poverty and universal unhappiness. It has made man worse than a beast. Do not be carried away by the external glitter of science. The ancient Rishis were our real well-wishers. Even now we claim ancestry to one or the other of these great ones. Yet we, take pride in decrying their wholesome teachings. This is not conducive to our welfare. Materialistic science can never bring about our real welfare and prosperity.

What did you learn from the mad behaviour of the eye patient? The low, bestial levels to which man has descended—this is what you see here. He cannot bear to see anyone rise higher than himself, anyone shine better than himself, anyone more prosperous than himself. He strives more to harm and vilify others than to promote his own welfare.

A beautiful utterance comes to my mind—"He is a great man who does good to others at the cost of his own welfare. He is a devil in human garb who harms others for his own good. He who harms others to no purpose—what to call this man we do not know." A large section of today's humanity belongs to this last abominable class. It is difficult to understand what the future condition will be when everyone is intent on harming everyone else. There could only be great chaos, misery and suffering everywhere.

And the wonder of wonders is that no one stops to think even for a moment. Everyone follows everyone else. Each man tries to outshine his neighbour. Every man follows a beaten track, blindly, without bestowing a thought whether he is doing the right thing or not.

A young man goes to school because his father went

250

to school and because his neighbour goes to school. He seeks employment because everyone seeks employment. He gets married because his father, grandfather and great grandfather got married. He earns wealth because everyone does so. He wastes his life because he does not know what else to do. Life to him has come to mean being born, begetting children, growing old, and then going to the grave. This is just like the story of Gandharvasen. When it died, one after another up to the king observed mourning. But the real seeker is not like that. He halts at every step and thinks. He is reflective. He does enquiry and gains discrimination. Then he abandons the worldly life and embraces the spiritual life. He is a wise man.

Such a wise Sadhaka takes to the practice of devotion, for, as we have seen in the story of the search for the greatest person, even the Lord is the real devotee's own.

When devotion and discrimination grow apace in the aspirant, he discovers that he had so long been wrongly identifying himself with the illusory covering sheaths—the body, the Prana, the mind, etc. He had an incorrect conception of his essential nature and of the nature of delusion that obstructs the realisation of this essential nature. That is what we learn from the story of the addicts of drugs.

Lastly, we learn from the story of the two lions that the grip of nescience over us is so strong and powerful, —like the lion's dread of the mysterious 'night'—that it needs a Guru, another lion, to point out to us our essential nature and to stand by as our support and guide while we roar 'Satchidananda Swarupoham'. The load of miseries and grief, delusion and despair, that we have so long been carrying—just as the lion was carrying the clothes of the washerman—drop away from us as we leap forward to reach our native abode of bliss.

Children, having successfully been through these soul-awakening experiences and having acquired a thorough knowledge of the nature of the world and the nature of spiritual life, you are really fit for initiation into the mysteries of Atma Jnana. Come, I will initiate you into the holy Order of Sannyas. And I pray to God to shower his blessings on you and bestow on you strength of will and enduring discrimination which will take you to the realms of immortal bliss!

76

HIDDEN TREASURE

THERE WAS ONCE a very poor family consisting of a husband, wife and a few children. They had to work hard to earn money for their food, and often went from market to market begging for a few coins or pieces of bread. Poor as they were, even the sight of money in the hands of the rich produced a thrill in their hearts. When they received a few small coins from kind-hearted people, they used to buy the bare necessities from the market and enjoy rest for a while on re-turning home. Often they had to go without food and comfort, lamenting over their miserable condition. They dwelt between tears and smiles, happiness and sorrow, gain and loss, pleasure and pain.

But in reality they had for their heritage a vast treasure of which they were completely unaware. It was buried in the ground where the cottage stood. They rested upon it, slept upon it, enjoyed the little they got and lived a miserable life, ignorant of their hereditary treasure. Had they dug into the ground, they would have found the treasure and ended their sorrow.

The same is the plight of the individual soul. Due to ignorance he is unaware of the supreme wealth of the

Atman which lies beneath the bed of his causal sheath or bliss sheath. He roams about in the process of worldly existence, enjoying sense-objects. Happiness is derived from the bliss sheath which has three mental modifications—Priya, Moda and Pramoda.

Priya is the delight of seeing the object of desire. Moda is the greater delight due to possessing the object of desire, and Pramoda is still greater delight due to the enjoyment of the object of desire. When the tension of the mind is released by the gradual satisfaction of a desire, the intellect of man turns inward to glimpse the bliss of the Atman through the veil of ignorance. If he rends asunder the veil, he will not be like the poor family, roaming about in the market of Samsara for the little happiness of sense-pleasure, which is mixed with so much humiliation, pain and affliction. Each day the individual soul, in the state of deep sleep, goes near the treasure, but due to the veil of ignorance, does not attain it.

When the Jiva digs the bed of ignorance with the spade of enquiry, into the real nature of the Self, with the strength of discrimination and dispassion, he recovers the hidden treasure of the Atman and thus becomes an Atma-Samrat or Self-monarch.

77

KRISHNA AND SUDAMA

WHEN SUDAMA came to meet Sri Krishna, the Lord was in the palace. Now Sudama was poorly dressed and was hesitating to go into the palace. Krishna at that time was with Radha. A guard entered saying, "Sire, a poor Brahmin in tattered garments and named Sudama has arrived and claims your honour as his dearest friend, and . . . "

Sri Krishna did not allow the guard to finish. The word "Sudama" was enough. Immediately, brushing aside the guard, He left His seat and ran out of the room crying, "Ah! Sudama! My dear Sudama!"

Radha was told nothing about Krishna's abrupt departure from the room and felt hurt. Presently, Krishna returned with Sudama. Seeing Radha sad, He remarked, "Radha, forgive me. The intensity of love that I bear for My Bhaktas is more than my very Self. I am their slave."

Then Sri Krishna gave Sudama the seat of honour, the seat of the Lord. While exchanging news, Krishna noticed a small parcel under Sudama's arm. This parcel contained a quantity of half-baked rice, which Sudama had brought as a present to the Lord. He was feeling shy to offer so small a present.

Krishna, however, snatched the parcel from under his arm and started putting into his mouth the baked rice, exclaiming: "Radha, never before did I taste such a delicious preparation."

Such is the great love that the Lord has for His devotees!

78

THE GRACE OF THE LORD

THE GRACE of the Lord is ever with His devotees, in all places and at all times. Even if you think of the Lord once, sincerely and with love from the bottom of your heart, He will rush towards you in times of danger and save you from peril. He becomes the servant of His Bhaktas. To Him the vows of His Bhaktas are greater than His own vows. The following story from the *Mahabharata* will reveal the love the Lord has for His Bhaktas.

The great war at Kurukshetra was in full progress. Karna had released the Nagastra, an Astra or powerful arrow that devours anything and everything. The Astra was aimed at Arjuna while he was immersed in the wondrous beauty of Lord Krishna's form. He did not see it coming towards him. It was about to pass right through his neck.

But Lord Krishna knew of this and the duty of saving His Bhakta fell upon Him. Even though He had taken the vow of not fighting or helping in the progress of the war, except to simply be the charioteer of Arjuna, Sri Krishna had to overlook His own vow to save His devotees, the Pandavas. By pressing the ground with His foot, Sri Krishna caused the chariot to be lowered.

This lowered the position of Arjuna's neck at which the Astra was aimed. When the Nagastra struck and tilted his crown, Arjuna came to his senses after being immersed in the beauty of Sri Krishna. Only then did he come to know how the Lord had saved him from the danger.

On the instruction of Krishna, when the Narayana Astra was released, the entire army of the Pandavas, as also Dharmaputra and Arjuna, bowed before it and were therefore saved.

But to Bhima, the mighty one, bowing to an enemy's Astra was a shameful act. He did not like the suggestion of Sri Krishna and was adamant and resolved to fight like a hero till life was extinct. The Lord knew the power of the Narayana Astra and also the danger that faced Bhima. Words would not influence him. So the Lord thought of an idea. Sri Krishna and Arjuna caused Bhima to prostrate on the ground by forcibly pushing him down, so that the Narayana Astra did not affect him.

Bhima did not prostrate on his own accord. Even so, the Lord is satisfied even if you prostrate before Him half-heartedly, for He knows that you are His Bhakta, something that you do not know. He knows fully well that even though you mechanically prostrate before Him today, you are sure to become His true Bhakta tomorrow. Once you turn to Him, He will become your servant forever, to save you from all dangers, just like He saved Bhima, Arjuna and the entire Pandava army.

Develop unswerving devotion to His Lotus Feet. Sing His Name and His glories. Ever live in His thoughts. Even if you ignore Him, He will not ignore you. He is your friend, well-wisher and benefactor.

May the Grace of the Almighty Lord be with you.

79

TIRUVALLUVAR'S WIFE

TIRUVALLUVAR, a Tamil saint of South India, one day put a shallow plate of water on the head of his wife and requested her to move along in a procession of dance, music and a variety of plays. He warned her that her head would be cut off if a single drop of water should fall to the ground.

The procession started from the front door of the grand temple of Sriranga, Trichnopoly. Tiruvalluvar's wife joined the group with the plate of water on her head. Her whole being was centred on the plate of water. The procession marched along four streets three times and at last terminated at the place of commencement. The woman managed to bring back the plate in entirety, without allowing a single drop of water to fall to the ground.

Tiruvalluvar asked his wife, "O Saraswathi Devi! did you hear the band, the music and play of the flute that accompanied the procession?"

She replied, "No."

"Did you see the fireworks?"

She again replied in the negative.

"Where was your mind then?"

"My lord, it was all on the plate of water. I knew

259

nothing, I heard nothing, I saw nothing, I remembered nothing. I had one strong and concentrated idea of the plate of water only."

"Now look here, Saraswathi! That must be the condition of your mind during meditation also. It is termed one-pointedness."

80

SAINTS ARE ONE AT HEART

HUNDREDS OF inspiring stories have gathered around the shining lives f Raghaviah and Nagore Andavan, the great contemporary saints of South India.

One was a Hindu, the other a Muslim. In their hearts was thè one Truth, in their minds was the one aim— the good of all. They were two in body but one in Him.

One Perumal Naidu's mangrove had, for the third year in succession, yielded not even a single fruit. Perumal had heard of Nagore Andavan's miraculous powers.

"If in the next season the garden should be fruitful, I shall offer the first mangoes to Sri Andavan," he resolved.

Nagore Andavan's Grace had forestalled time itself! A few days after he took the resolve, and entirely out of season, the mango trees blossomed. A month later, when no one would have dreamt of getting a mango, the trees were heavily laden with fruits. Imagine Perumal's joy and wonderment!

True to his promise he resolved to take the first dozen fruits to Nagore Andavan, to whose Grace alone he ascribed the miraculous fruition of the garden. His faith now was so great that he wanted to travel the distance of forty miles to the saint by foot as a pilgrimage.

There were yet seven miles to reach the saint. A poor beggar who was resting peacefully beneath a tree, hailed Perumal.

"What are you carrying? Mangoes? Give me one."

Perumal was surprised that the Sadhu had divined what he was carrying; but he was unwilling to part with even one of the mangoes intended for Nagore Andavan. He took no notice of the Sadhu's request.

Nagore Andavan was difficult to find that day. It needed a full hour's search to find him sitting beneath a tree. Perumal placed the precious load at the feet of the saint.

"Prabho! I seek Thy Grace." He explained his vow and its fulfilment.

Andavan turned his face away!

"Hum! When you were asked to give the fruits, you refused. Now you want me to accept them. Take them back. Who wants them?"

Perumal was puzzled. In his mind flashed the truth—he understood. Without a further word, he ran back seven miles. The Sadhu, no other than Raghaviah, was still there. Perumal fell at his feet.

"Pardon me, Maharaj. I knew not."

"Never mind. You can leave the whole lot with me."

The Jivanmukta chided him not for his previous misbehaviour. He took nothing as an insult. The God-man who had attained immortal bliss was unaffected; he delighted in everything that happened.

Perumal returned home supremely happy at the revelation of the unity of saints.

81

STORIES THAT TRANSFORM

A FATHER AND son once went to a fair. The son got lost in the crowd. Everyone was talking and making a great noise. The father listened intently to catch his son's voice. He knew that his son was there in the crowd. Eventually he was able to recognise his voice, though it was very much distorted by the noise of the crowd. He followed the source of the voice and discovered his son.

The father is the individual soul and the son is the Atman. The Self is "hidden" in the various objects of the world. Its Presence is felt by the wise soul in moments of deep reflection. If the Atman did not exist at all, then all attempts to realise It would be futile. If the Atman alone existed, without the veiling sheaths, there would be no need for doing Sadhana to attain It. Through the sheaths, through the objects of the world, the light of the Self, the bliss of the Atman, the peace of the Eternal, shine now and then, but grossly distorted by the deceptive Maya. The wise individual recognises this, follows It with one-pointed mind and finally reaches the fountain-source of light, peace and bliss— the Self, which is infinite and immortal.

THE BEST CHOICE

A millionaire left a will. He had several sons. He said in the will: "Let each of my sons choose one thing that he desires most. The rest of my estate shall go to the best of my slaves."

The court of law asked the sons to choose whatever they wanted. One chose a palace, another a costly jewel, a third wanted a garden.

The turn of the last son came. He rose and said, "Sir, I choose my father's slave."

Everyone was puzzled. What a poor choice!

But no, by choosing this one slave, the young man had automatically become the owner of the entire property left over after the other sons had been satisfied. Because by law the slave's property belongs to his master, the young man automatically became the owner of the entire property plus the faithful slave.

Similar is the case with the wise aspirant. He aspires for the lowliest position, the humblest life, the simplest attire. In serving the poor, the sick and the suffering, he finds his delight. In them he sees the Lord. And what does he get? He attains union with the Lord of the universe. He becomes the master of all spiritual wealth. Is there anything greater than this? But those who choose the petty things of the world, the ephemeral sense-objects, waste their lives away and gain nothing worthwhile.

Aspire for God-realisation. You will then obtain the highest wealth of Cosmic Consciousness. Then everything else will be added unto this attainment.

SERVICE OF SAINTS

Lord Krishna playfully entered the house of a cowherd. This Gopa at once locked the door and said to

Krishna, "O Lord! You are now caught. Please bless me. Place your divine palm on my head. I will attain liberation. Then only will I let you go"

However much Krishna tried, the Gopa refused even to entertain the thought that Krishna was only a cowherd.

The Lord was pleased. He blessed the Gopa. The Gopa at once said, "Bhagawan, please place your hand on that pot also."

The Lord playfully did so. At once a deer jumped out and fell at the feet of the Lord; the deer also attained liberation.

In his previous birth the Gopa was a Maharishi. He had a deer which ate of his leavings and was highly devoted to him. When he departed from this world, the deer prayed to him, "Maharishi, please grant me also release from this Samsara. If you remember me, you can do so. You are going to take birth as the Lord's playmate in your next birth. I will be born as a pot in your house. Please secure the Lord's blessings for me also."

The Maharishi promised. The next birth was their last birth.

Serve the saints. Be devoted to them. Whether you have other qualifications or not, you will attain liberation when they get their liberation.

WE ARE HIS RESPONSIBILITY

A party of six people were having a pleasure ride in a motor-boat near the Bombay harbour. Suddenly the weather changed and the sea was turbulent. Several people in the boat grew panic-stricken, but one Sikh alone remained unperturbed.

An Anglo-Indian woman, who was greatly worried

over her safety, was annoyed to see the Sikh sitting apparently without the least worry, with a serene smile playing on his face.

"Are you mad?" she asked. "The boat is about to sink and you are sitting there as though nothing is happening."

"Mother," replied the Sikh, "did we create ourselves? No. Someone—God—has created us. Does He not have the power to protect us? Is He not protecting us? Who is responsible for our lives? It is God. Who feeds us daily? God. Who makes the breath flow in our nostrils? It is God. Who enables us to digest our food? Who makes our hearts pump blood? God. We are His responsibility. His Will be done, mother. Fear not. He will protect us."

"Fool!" exclaimed the Anglo-Indian woman, "your foolishness is surely going to land you at the bottom of the sea. Come, be wise, put the life-belt on and jump with us. We will float along till someone rescues us."

The Sikh looked away, apparently deeply immersed in thought. The Anglo-Indian lady jumped off the boat with some others. They were promptly seized by a shark which had a good meal of them. Tossed about on the waves, the motor-boat danced its way safely to the shore with the Sikh and a few others. The co-passengers of the Sikh greatly admired his faith in God and became his followers.

MADA-DEVATA'S TRICK

Lobeswar was rolling in wealth. He had inherited great wealth and he lived for accumulating wealth alone. He had no other thought. There was no unrighteous act he did not do to acquire and accumulate wealth. He robbed and ill-treated many for money.

Lobeswar's sons died one by one. He had no one in the world to look after him. He was growing old. The villagers cheated him, robbed him of his wealth and despised him. In despair he resorted to the worship of a Tamasic Deity, Mada-Devata, outside his village. He had the firm feeling that the Mada-Devata was the highest Divinity, the Supreme Brahman Himself.

Lobeswar fell gravely ill. The villagers merely laughed at him. He was confident that the Mada-Devata would save him. A few minutes before his death, the Mada-Devata took him bodily to Benares by its magic powers. He died at Benares with the Rama-Mantra on his lips and attained liberation. God, whom Lobeswar had worshipped through the Mada-Devata, had in His own very mysterious way saved him.

Whatever Devata you worship, feel that it is the Supreme Brahman. You will surely attain liberation.

THE STORY OF THE CONCH

Jealousy is the essential nature of Maya. This trait is everywhere. There is a beautiful story to illustrate that a jealous man loses in the end, and that one loses even a good boon by misuse due to jealousy.

A man once obtained a conch by worshipping a certain Deity. It could fulfil all his desires when it was blown, but at the same time his neighbour would get double the benefit.

The man blew the conch, desiring a mansion. At once he obtained a beautiful mansion to live in, but his neighbour got two mansions. Again he blew the conch, desiring an elephant. He got it, but his neighbour obtained two elephants.

The owner of the conch became jealous of his neighbour. He did not want him to be benefited. So he again blew the conch with the desire that he should lose one eye. The neighbour and his family lost both their eyes. When they came out of their house they fell into a well and got drowned as they were blind. They lost their lives on account of the jealousy of the man.

Coming to know of these events, the Deity snatched the conch away from the hands of the jealous man and admonished him severely.

The story teaches us that one should give up jealousy, as it is one of the Shad-ripus mentioned in our *Shastras*. One should desire the welfare of all. Jealousy is a terrible canker that ruins one completely. It destroys all peace, holiness and merit. It deludes one and makes one completely blind.

THE STORY OF GRIEF

A landlord had built a fine bungalow at a cost of Rs. 4,000. It was the fruit of his savings over a number of years. He himself planned the house and had it built under his personal supervision. Now he suddenly began dreaming every night that the house had crumbled down. He was very worried and consulted the astrologers. They too confirmed that the building would not stand. There was no limit to his grief.

His shrewd wife gave him an idea. He sold the house for Rs. 4,000. With the crisp hundred-rupee notes, he went to live in a rented hut. He slept happily that night and woke up the next morning to hear that some mischief-mongers had set fire to his old house and that it had been reduced to rubble. He himself went over to the house and watched the spectacle with not a trace of grief. He was inwardly happy that he had sold it in time. The house was no longer his. He remembered the forty hundred-rupee notes in his money-box—*his* money. He ran back to his house.

The nightmares returned. Thoughts of robbers kept him awake at night. He suspected his own brothers and even his sons. His wife came to his rescue again. On her advice he deposited the money in the State Bank and got the receipt. The next day there was a daring bank robbery and it was reported that all the money had been stolen. But our landlord was not worried; he had his receipt with him.

Fear once again began to haunt him. The thought that his sons might poison him and claim the money from the bank with the receipt, began to obsess him.

A holy man from the village came to him one day and pleaded for help to run the orphanage that had been established there. Taking that as the command of the Lord, the good landlord at once went in, brought the receipt and handed it over to the Sadhu as his contribution to the orphanage. A building was constructed in the orphanage in the name of the landlord. His reputation as a noble, generous man spread far and wide. People held him in high esteem. He had no fear now. He knew that, so long as he was alive, the people around him would make him happy and that he could live in peace. He also knew that when he left this world, the charity and prayers of the orphans would stand him in good stead in the other world.

Attachment brings grief. What you consider "mine" turns into your own enemy. From it springs all grief. When you detach yourself from an object, it ceases to worry you. Cut at the root of attachment. Treat everything as His. You will enjoy peace and happiness.